THE
WEEKEND
QUILTER

FABULOUS QUILTS
TO MAKE IN A WEEKEND

THE WEEKEND QUILTER

FABULOUS QUILTS TO MAKE IN A WEEKEND

Edited by Rosemary Wilkinson

Reader's Digest

The Reader's Digest Association, Inc.
Pleasantville, New York/Montreal

A Reader's Digest Book
This edition first published in the UK in 1997 by
New Holland (Publishers) Ltd

Created and produced by Rosemary Wilkinson Publishing
Art editor: Sara Kidd
Illustrator: Carol Hill
Photographer: Marie-Louise Avery
Copy editor: Michèle Clarke
Reproduction by cmyk prepress

Copyright © 1997 in text New Holland (Publishers) Ltd
Copyright © 1997 in photographs New Holland (Publishers) Ltd
Copyright © 1997 in illustrations New Holland (Publishers) Ltd
Copyright © 1997 in quilt designs Pauline Adams, Jenni Dobson, Carol Dowsett, Gill Turley and Anne Walker

All rights reserved. Unauthorized reproduction, in any manner, is prohibited.

Library of Congress Cataloging in Publication Data
The weekend quilter / edited by Rosemary Wilkinson.
    p.   cm.
    Includes index.
    ISBN 0-89577-995-1
    1. Patchwork–Patterns.   2. Quilting–Patterns.   3. Patchwork quilts.
   I. Wilkinson, Rosemary.
   TT835.W42   1997
   746.46'041—dc21   97-18504

Reader's Digest and the Pegasus logo are registered trademarks of
The Reader's Digest Association, Inc.
Printed in Singapore

CONTRIBUTOR PROFILES

PAULINE ADAMS
was one of the team operating The Quilters' Guild of Great Britain's quilt documentation program and contributed to the resulting book, *Quilt Treasures*. She has written a number of articles in *The Quilter* magazine and her own book on patchwork. She exhibits regularly at national and local shows.

JENNI DOBSON
is a regular contributor to national patchwork magazines and has been teaching and demonstrating patchwork at major European events since the late 1970s. Her quilts have won rosettes at major British quilt shows and were selected by The Quilters' Guild for their fourth and fifth national exhibitions.

CAROL DOWSETT
has taught City & Guild Creative Studies Patchwork courses for many years. As a founding member of The Computer Textile Design Group, she has been involved in developing the use of computers for design into textiles in secondary schools. Her computer-designed hangings are exhibited nationally and throughout Europe.

GILL TURLEY
works as a freelance lecturer and teacher of quiltmaking. The Quilters' Guild selected her quilts to include in their national exhibitions in 1987, 1991, and 1993 and photographs of her quilts have been featured in several recent quilt books. She has been a member of the executive committee of The Quilters' Guild since 1991.

ANNE WALKER
originally trained as a mathematics teacher and has always had a great interest in geometric designs. She is a prominent member of The Quilters' Guild. She has been involved in setting up the curriculum for a national patchwork course and has written and contributed to other patchwork books. She currently runs a patchwork and quilting supplies business, Piecemakers.

CONTENTS

QUICK QUILT TECHNIQUES 6
Anne Walker

QUICK QUILT TECHNIQUES

DEVELOPMENT OF TECHNIQUES

The art of quiltmaking has been with us for many generations. Quiltmaking techniques were first brought to British shores by the Crusaders, who found them much in use in the Middle East. By the time of the Victorian era quilting was an established art form in many households. It was at this time that the skilled needlewoman demonstrated that she was indeed an artist and a designer, piecing together intricate designs from an array of wonderful fabrics. Much of the patchwork done at this time was either the rich "crazy patchwork" in sumptuous fabrics, embellished with stitches and beads, or geometric piecing, simple geometric shapes stitched over papers before being joined together with a whipstitch. This latter method has come to be known as "English paper piecing."

In America pioneer women developed a technique that has become an American art form, the "patchwork block"; this enables quiltmakers to piece their quilts in small units before assembling the quilt top. The revival of patchwork in Britain in the 1970s was very much based on these blockmaking techniques.

If we look at many patchwork quilt patterns they can be broken down into smaller units consisting of strips, squares, and triangles. For decades these shapes have been cut using templates and pieced either by hand or machine. Such templates have been an invaluable tool for the patchworker, and indeed still are when more intricate shapes are used. However, modern lifestyles often demand a quicker approach. The advent of the rotary cutter has enabled the process to be speeded up, allowing the quiltmaker to achieve pleasing results in much shorter time, for example, in just a weekend. All the quilts in this book are quick projects in which the pieces are cut with a rotary cutter and machine pieced. They allow the reader to be creative in the time available, however short.

QUILT SIZES

A favorite and versatile quilt size is between 54 and 60 in/135 and 155 cm square, which can be used for a baby – as a wrap, a play rug, crib quilt, and even for a while as a single-bed quilt – or for an adult as a lap quilt. Larger square quilts can be used as throws. The book also features rectangular quilts for use as baby carriage and crib quilts, single-bed quilts, throws, or as elegant wall hangings.

FABRICS
Selection

Selecting fabric for a project is a personal thing. Each of the projects included is made in the maker's own choice, and it is clear to see that a quiltmaker will develop a unique style and taste. Some projects are made from soft flannels and brushed cottons to produce warm and comforting quilts, others are made from cottons, resulting in bright color arrangements suitable for display or for interior decorations. In each of the five sections suggestions have been given for using different color schemes for one of the quilts.

Your fabric choice will stamp your individuality on the project. It is never possible to recreate a quilt exactly, as fabric designs and color schemes are always changing. To achieve interest in your quilt you need to use different tonal values, and if you are using print fabrics, the scale of the print is also an important factor. The tonal values of fabric in your quilt should include light, medium, and dark fabrics. These values are relative to each other, so one person's medium may be another person's light; the fabrics can even play different roles in the same quilt. If you are unsure of the value of the fabrics, you can view them through a value finder, a red screen that eliminates the color and allows you to see the lightness and darkness, i.e., the value. A similar effect can be achieved by photocopying fabric and looking at the value of the grayness. Another technique that you can employ is to stare at the fabric selection and gradually squint at it: the darker fabrics "disappear" first. This is a good technique when perhaps you are confused between brightness and lightness.

Equipment for the quick quilter: an acrylic ruler; a bias square; a set square; a rotary cutter and mat; a "BiRangle™"; a hand-held hoop; various marking pencils and quilting threads and a selection of fabric pieces.

The scale of the design of a print fabric is very important. Your quilt needs to hold interest both close to and from a distance. Try to use a variety of scales – small prints when viewed from the distance will look like solids. Geometric designs add movement, encouraging the eye to move over the surface and allowing you to see the other fabrics. There are also fabrics on the market that are monochromatic prints or textured solids, which are good substitutes for a solid fabric, giving a softer overall finished look.

You can always experiment with coloring a quilt design on paper before making your fabric selection, but remember, no colored pencil or felt-tip pen can re-create a single fabric or its effect when placed next to another. If you are unsure of your fabric selection, purchase only a small amount and try a fabric mock-up. Quiltmakers are avid collectors of fabric, often buying without a project in mind. These fabrics can be used for some of the projects in this book; if, however, you plan to purchase additional fabrics, take the existing ones along with you to see them all together, as it is very difficult to carry an image of color in your head. Finally, always be prepared to change your mind.

All the fabric sizes in this book give a margin for error, so that you can purchase fabric with confidence. Most rotary cutting projects involve the cutting of strips first; these are best cut from across the width of fabric. Therefore, take care if a design calls for a quarter: most quilting supply shops sell quarters either "fat" or "long." A long quarter is cut 9 in/25 cm deep by the width of the bolt. A fat quarter is cut 18 in/50 cm deep by the width of the bolt, then split at the fold to give a piece 18 x 22 in/50 x 56 cm. Only buy a fat quarter if the design specifies such a size.

Preparation

All the fabric for your project must be washed separately to ensure that excess dye is removed. You do not need a detergent but the water needs to be hot. Keep rinsing until the water runs clear, which may take several rinses. If you wish to use the washing machine and have no means of collecting the waste water to check for dye, place a piece of white cloth in the machine together with the fabric. If the dye bleeds, it will do so into the white cloth. Repeat the process until no more dye runs. If dye continues to run after repeated washes, you may feel that you have to abandon this fabric. It is not advisable to try setting the dye with salt or vinegar, as it will only set it until the next wash and if you intend to wash your quilt, the color will run throughout the quilt. Separate instructions are given within the book for fabric preparation if you are dyeing it yourself.

After washing, partially dry, then iron the fabric while it is still damp to replace its original crispness. Press with the selvages together just as it came off the bolt.

Fabric preparation is not included in the overall timing of the quilts given in the introduction to each one. Timing begins once you start cutting the fabrics.

ROTARY CUTTING
Equipment

There are lots of different pieces of rotary cutting equipment on the market. You will need the following basic set for the quilts in this book:

Acrylic rotary ruler. This should be a rotary ruler with a nonbeveled edge. Never use metal rulers, as they will ruin the blades of your rotary cutter. Markings should be on the underside of the ruler and should be laser printed and easy to read. Beware of any ruler with the markings on the top surface; this leads to an altered view of the measurements, which will not be accurate. Any angles marked on the ruler should be marked in both directions. A good size of ruler to have is 6 x 24 in/ 15 x 60 cm.

Bias square. This special tool will aid the cutting and squaring up of half square triangle units. A good size to have is 6 x 6 in/ 15 x 15 cm.

BiRangle™. This tool (see page 143) is marked with a grid designed to help you to stitch rectangles twice as long as they are wide. When the rectangles are cut from contrasting strips that have been stitched together, you can quickly and accurately make long, thin pairs of triangles.

Rotary cutter. This comes in different sizes: small, medium, and large. A good size to have is the medium, which is classed as heavy duty. The small one is good for trimming and for cutting curves. The large one is excellent for cutting large multiple layers, but if you are a newcomer to the technique, this is slightly more difficult to control. Cutters come with a safety cover that should be engaged at all times when you are not cutting. Replacement blades are readily available. Keep your cutter well maintained: blunt blades will ruin your mat as well as making cutting difficult and unpleasant. Also make sure that cutters are stored safely, out of reach of children. Safe habits prevent accidents from happening.

Self-healing rotary cutting mat This is essential. Do not cut on any other surface. The mats come in a variety of sizes: a good size is one on which the fabric will fit with only one fold. The mats come with a grid on one side. This grid is roller printed and is not always accurate, so do not rely on it for measurements. To avoid confusion you could always use the reverse side of the mat.

Set square. This is for straightening up the fabric before cutting. A second rotary cutting ruler will substitute for this.

All this equipment, except for the BiRangle™, is available with either U.S. imperial or metric measurements.

Measurements

All measurements are given in both U.S. imperial and metric equivalents. Fabric allowances are interchangeable for the purpose of buying the required fabric. However, all cutting instructions are not. Use either U.S. imperial or metric measurements: do not mix the two.

The seam allowances (unless otherwise stated) are ¼ in if you are working in U.S. imperial measures or 0.75 cm if working in metric. Although 0.75 cm is bigger than ¼ in, these seam allowances work well with the rotary cutting equipment. All cutting instructions already include seam allowances, therefore you will not need to add any extra. However, if you adapt any of the quilts or create your own designs, it is worth remembering the following when calculating seam allowances:

U.S. Imperial
seam allowance: ¼ in
cutting strips/squares/rectangles: add ½ in
cutting half-square triangles: add ⅞ in
cutting quarter-square triangles: add 1¼ in

Metric
seam allowance: 0.75 cm
cutting strips/squares/rectangles: add 1.5 cm
cutting half-square triangles: add 2.5 cm
cutting quarter-square triangles: add 3.5 cm

See below to find out how these are calculated.

finished size: ¼ + ⅝ = ⅞ in
0.75 + 1.75 = 2.5 cm

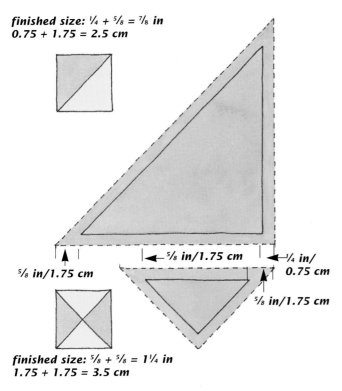

⅝ in/1.75 cm

← ⅝ in/1.75 cm →   ←¼ in/ 0.75 cm

⅝ in/1.75 cm

finished size: ⅝ + ⅝ = 1¼ in
1.75 + 1.75 = 3.5 cm

Creating a straight edge

Regardless of how well the fabric was originally cut, you will have to straighten the edge before cutting pieces for your quilt in order to produce accurate strips across the fabric.

1 Place your fabric on the cutting mat with the fold toward you and the selvage away from you and all the surplus fabric to the side in the direction of the hand you cut with. Make sure that the selvages are exactly aligned.

2 Lay a set square on the fold of the fabric and line your ruler up against the square with a horizontal line on the ruler in line with the bottom of the square (shown below).

3 Place your hand at the bottom of the ruler, remove the set square and, starting cutting in front of the fold in the fabric, cut until your cutter is level with the top of your hand, then, maintaining the pressure on the cutter, creep your hand farther up the ruler, cut again and repeat the process until you have finished cutting off the waste strip (shown below).

Cutting strips

This is the first stage to producing strips cut crosswise across the fabric, either to be used as they are or to be cut again to produce squares, rectangles, and triangles.

1 Keep the fold in the fabric after creating a straight edge, and fold the fabric in half again, so that the fold lies on top of the selvages and the cut edges lie together (shown below). There are now four thicknesses of fabric.

2 Place the ruler on your fabric with a horizontal line on the fold and the desired width measurement on the straightened edge (shown below).

3 Place your hand firmly in the center of the ruler. Start cutting before the fold and cut across the fabric in one movement.

4 Repeat until you have cut the number of strips needed. Open out the strips and check that they have straight edges. If they have a slight V shape, or if it becomes difficult to line up the ruler with the horizontal on the fold and the measurement along the whole cut edge, repeat the process to create a straight edge given on page 9.

Cutting squares

1 Cut strips to the desired width as previously described.

2 Pick up a strip with the double fold in your cutting hand and turn until it is horizontal on the board. Straighten up the end with the single fold and selvage (shown below).

3 Using the same width measurement as the strip, cut it into squares, making sure a horizontal line on the ruler is on the bottom edge of the fabric (shown below). This process is called **subcutting**.

Cutting rectangles

1 Cut strips to the width of one of the measurements of the desired rectangle as described above.

2 Turn the strip for cutting again, straighten the end and subcut using the second measurement of the desired rectangle.

Cutting measurements wider than ruler

A second ruler or square can be used to aid the cutting of wider strips (shown below).

Cutting half-square triangles

1 Cut strips to the desired measurement, including the seam allowances.

2 Turn the strip for subcutting as before, straighten the end and cut a square.

3 Pivot the ruler until it lies exactly across the diagonal of the square. Cut into triangles (shown below).

4 Repeat steps 2 and 3 until you have subcut the required number of half-square triangles.

Cutting quarter-square triangles

1 Cut strips to the desired measurement, including the seam allowances.

2 Turn the strip for subcutting as before, straighten the end and cut a square.

3 Pivot the ruler until it lies exactly across one diagonal of the square and cut.

4 Without moving the pieces, pivot the ruler the other way until it lies exactly across the other diagonal of the square, and cut (shown below).

5 Repeat steps 2 to 4 until you have subcut the required number of quarter-square triangles.

Cutting stitched strips

1 Lay the strips across the mat with the surplus length toward the hand you cut with.

2 This time when trimming or subcutting, line up a horizontal line on the ruler with one of the seams instead of with the lower edge of the fabric.

MACHINE STITCHING
Preparation

Start each quilt with a new needle. If you will be subcutting stitched strips, the stitch length needs to be shorter than for normal stitching. A guide is to stitch at 12 stitches to the inch/ 5 stitches to the centimeter.

For an accurate quilt top, the seam allowance that you stitch must also be accurate; you cannot just trust in the width of your presser foot. To ensure an accurate width, work as follows:

1 Take a piece of graph paper either marked in quarter inches or in millimeters and cut the right-hand edge of the paper so that you have a line exactly ¼ in/0.75 cm from the edge.

2 Place this paper under the presser foot and stitch along the line.

3 Stick a piece of masking tape on the bed of your machine along the edge of the paper. (Alternatively there are magnetic stitching guides that you can place on the machine up against the edge of the paper.)

4 Remove the paper and you are ready to stitch. It is always advisable to stitch a test piece first. Cut three short pieces of fabric 1½ in/4.5 cm wide. Stitch the three strips together along the long sides into a block, butting the fabric against your stitching guide. Press the seams away from the center strip, then measure between the seam lines on the right side. If you are accurate, this measurement will be 1 in/3 cm. If it is in any way off, set up your guide again and retest.

Piecing

Machine piecing always appears to use an endless supply of thread, so before starting a project, fill several bobbins in readiness.

Chain piecing is a method that speeds up the whole process: stitch two pieces together, leave them under the presser foot, then butt up the next pair. Continue stitching and butting up the following pairs until you have stitched all the pieces (shown below, left).

A third piece can be added to these two in the same way (shown below, right) and the process can be repeated as often as you like. Snip the pieces apart when you have finished.

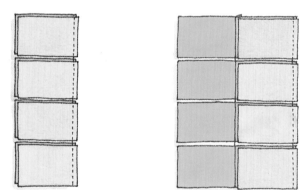

When machine piecing, the meeting of seams can, if tackled wrongly, become too bulky. Pressing instructions are given with individual projects; following these will ensure that the seams nest neatly together.

Taming seam crossings is necessary where seams meet in the middle of a pinwheel, otherwise they will form a nasty lump. If the seams all lie in the same direction, the lump goes. To enable the last seam stitched to lie similarly, undo a few stitches within the seam allowance of the the two seams at right angles to it. Do this carefully, being sure not to undo nearer the seam allowance than one stitch. Trim off any projecting triangle points and press.

Pressing is an important part of machine piecing. It must be done as you go along, and not left to the end, as is often the case with hand piecing.

Seams can be finger pressed first; this is when the seam is pushed over and squeezed between your thumb and finger. The work can then be pressed with an iron both on the wrong and the right sides to ensure that no pleats are pressed in. Always press in the direction of the grain and not across the bias, which will stretch the pieces.

ADDING BORDERS
Borders with butted edges

These borders are the easiest and quickest to stitch, and if this is your first quilt, they are probably preferable. Although some of the projects in the book give measurements for the borders, always check the measurements of your quilt top before cutting these long strips.

1 To determine the length of the side borders, measure center top to center bottom of the quilt. Cut two borders of this length by the required width.

2 Pin to the side edges, adjusting the quilt top to fit as necessary, then stitch using an exact ¼ in/0.75 cm seam allowance. Press the seam toward the border.

3 Once the side borders have been stitched, measure the work again, this time from center side to center side. This determines the length of the top and bottom borders. Cut two border strips this length.

4 Pin and stitch to the top and bottom edges of the quilt. Press toward the border. If more than one border is required, simply repeat the process.

Borders with mitered corners

These borders take a bit more time but give a professional finish to your quilt.

1 Determine the length and width of your quilt top by measuring from center top to center bottom and from center side to center side.

2 Cut border pieces to these measurements plus twice the width of the border plus approximately 2 in/5 cm extra for the seam allowance.

3 Pin a border strip to the quilt edge, matching the strip center to the quilt edge center. Allow the excess border fabric to extend beyond each end.

4 Stitch to the quilt edge using an exact ¼ in/0.75 cm seam allowance, starting and finishing ¼ in/0.75 cm from the corner (shown below).

5 Repeat with the remaining borders. Press the seam allowances toward the borders.

6 To form the miters, lay the quilt wrong side up, then either press the borders (shown below, left), match the folds, pin and stitch, finishing at the inner corner, or overlap the corners (shown below, right) and place the 45° line of your rotary ruler on the raw edge of the border. Pencil a line from the border seam to the outside edge. Overlap the adjacent border and mark again.

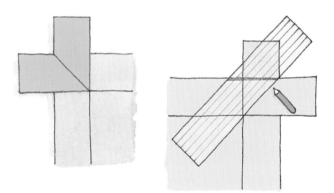

7 With right sides together, match the drawn lines, pin and stitch along the marked line (shown below).

8 Check the right side, then trim to ¼ in/0.75 cm. Press this seam allowance open. Whichever method you choose, repeat on the remaining three corners.

QUILTING

The primary function of the quilting stitches is to hold the three layers of the quilt (top, batting, and backing) together securely enough to last the lifetime of the quilt. Traditional hand quilting can be a slow process; therefore, on the quilts featured in this book the quilting is either by machine or there are suggestions for quick hand-quilting designs. You can always change from machine to hand quilting if time is not a factor.

Marking quilting designs

Designs can be as complicated or as simple as you wish. If you intend to machine quilt, look for designs that can be stitched in a continuous motion. Quick quilting designs make use of seam lines or the pattern on the fabric. Any other designs need to be marked before the quilt is layered.

There are a variety of marking tools available: 2H pencils, silver and yellow quilters' pencils, washable marking pens, etc. Whichever you choose, always test the marker on a scrap of the fabric you have used in your quilt; you should be able to remove your designs after you have quilted.

The quilt top then needs to be attached to the backing and batting, by either bagging out or layering.

Bagging out

This is a quick method that neatens the edges of a quilt in place of adding a binding.

1 Lay the batting out on a flat surface. Lay the backing fabric on top of the batting, right side up, then lay the quilt top, right side down, on top.

2 Trim the backing fabric and the batting to the same size as the quilt top all round. Take care not to cut into the quilt top when doing this.

3 Pin the layers together, then stitch round the edges, leaving an opening long enough to turn the quilt through (shown below).

4 Trim the batting close to the seam line, then turn the quilt through, so that the batting is in the center of the sandwich. Slipstitch the opening closed.

5 Baste with thread or safety pins ready for quilting as described below.

Layering

The backing and batting should be slightly bigger all round than the quilt top.

1 Lay out the backing fabric right side down, smooth out and stretch taut. If possible, stick the edge at intervals with masking tape. Lay the batting on the top of the backing and the quilt top on the top of the batting with right side up.

2 Pin the layers together starting from the center and working out, keeping the fabrics smooth.

Basting

This is necessary to hold the three layers securely together all over the quilt so that the fabrics don't wrinkle when quilted. It can be done with thread or safety pins.

1 When using thread, take long pieces of thread, start in the middle, and baste out to the edge in rows in both directions (shown below).

2 When using safety pins, these should be placed all over the quilt at intervals no greater than a hand's width in any one direction. Use short, fine, rustless pins to avoid permanently marking the quilt.

3 Short plastic tags are also available that can be shot through the quilt with a basting gun instead of using safety pins.

Machine quilting

When a quilt is machine quilted, a continuous line of thread is visible on both the top and the back of the quilt; you need, therefore, to choose a lightweight thread to work with. Threads are numbered in such a way that the lighter the thread, the higher the number. Before quilting your project, make up a sample sandwich of backing, batting and top fabrics as used in the quilt and try different threads to achieve the effect that you like. You can even choose an invisible thread if you wish.

Machine needles are numbered 70/10, 80/12, 90/14, etc. The finer the needle, the lower the number: 70/10 or 80/12 are suitable for both piecing and quilting with lightweight or invisible thread.

A walking or even-feed foot is essential to prevent tucks forming in the quilt top or backing. This foot is used with the feed dogs up and therefore is the best technique for designs with continuous, fairly straight lines. You can turn wide curves and pivot, but you cannot turn tight curves. It is used for stitching in the ditch, simple outline stitching, and stitching in a grid design. For tight curves or freehand quilting, you will need to use the darning foot with the feed dogs down.

When you are using a walking or even-feed foot, the machine controls the direction and the stitch length. In general, the stitch length needs to be longer than for regular stitching. To start and end a line of quilting, set the stitch length to very short and stitch about eight stitches, then snip off the loose threads close to the surface of the quilt.

Quilting in the ditch

One of the simplest, and therefore most popular, methods of machine-quilting is quilting in-the-ditch. When a top is pieced and pressed all the seams have a low side with no seam allowance underneath: this is the ditch. The quilting is done on this side close to the seam.

Freehand quilting

With this method you control the direction and the length of the stitches by moving the quilt forward, backward, and sideways under the needle of the sewing machine. You will need much practice to achieve perfect results.

Hand quilting

To hand quilt you need to select a stronger thread than that used for normal stitching. There are several brands of quilting thread on the market. Choose a color of quilting thread that will either blend or contrast with the fabrics for the top and backing; the choice is yours. If you wish, you can use different colors in the same quilt. Special needles called "betweens" are used, and you need to select a 9, 10, or 12. The larger the number, the smaller the needle. The quilt top needs to be held flat either in a frame or in a hoop.

Frame

Some floor frames do not require the quilt to be basted; the layers are held together by the frame.

1 Baste the backing fabric, wrong side up, to the tape that is fixed to the front and back rollers of the frame. Roll the excess backing fabric onto the back roller until the fabric in the frame is taut.

2 Attach the bottom edge of the batting to the backing fabric along the front roller only, using long basting stitches. Smooth the batting toward the back of the frame.

3 Arrange the quilt top over the batting; baste through all three layers along the front edge only.

4 To hold the batting and quilt top in position along the far edge of the frame, use long, fine pins or needles. The batting and quilt top hang loose over the back roller.

5 Quilt the area in front of you, then release the tension and roll more backing off the back roller. Wind the quilted part onto the front roller, retension, and continue to quilt.

Hoop

Hoops can be hand held (round and oval) or on a floor stand. If you are using a hand-held hoop, choose a 14 in/35 cm or 16 in/40 cm diameter for ease. Hoops on floor stands can have a bigger diameter. Hoops are considered to be more portable, and they allow you to turn the work. Do not leave a quilt in a hoop when you are not working on it, as this will distort your piece.

Layer and baste the quilt, then place the quilt over the bottom ring and place the top ring over the quilt. Tighten the ring: the fabric need not be as tight as a drumhead, but the work should be smooth. Work from the center outward.

Simple scroll frames are also available which will allow you the portability of a hoop while working with a frame.

The quilting process

The goal in hand quilting is to form straight, even stitches with the same size space in between as the length of the stitches showing.

1 Cut a length of thread about 18 in/45 cm long and tie a single knot in the end cut from the spool.

2 To start quilting, enter the work with a flat knot about ¾ in/ 2 cm from where you want to start quilting, run the needle through the batting only and come up at the starting point. Pull the thread sharply and the knot will pop through the surface and lodge in the batting.

3 To quilt, the needle needs to enter the fabric at a perpendicular angle. Hold the needle between your thumb and forefinger and place the point where you wish to form the first stitch. Push the needle through the quilt so that it only just pierces the undersurface, then lodge the eye of the needle in the end of your thimble. The end of your forefinger under the quilt will just feel the tip of the needle. Some quilters like to wear a second thimble or some other protection on the finger of their underneath hand.

4 The underneath finger pushes upward at the same time as the thimble rocks the eye end of the needle toward the surface of the quilt. The point of the needle will reappear through the top.

5 Rock the needle with the thimble into a perpendicular position and reenter the fabric.

6 Repeat until you have a few stitches on the needle. Pull the thread through and repeat the process (shown below).

7 To finish off, quilt until you have about 6 in/15 cm of thread left, then make a knot by passing the needle around the thread to form a loop and passing the needle through the loop. Pull the loop to the surface of the quilt and tighten to form a knot. Take one more stitch and pop the knot through the surface. Take the needle through the batting and back through the surface of the quilt, pull the thread taut, then cut off close to the surface.

TYING A QUILT

A quick alternative to quilting is tying. By this method the top, batting, and backing sandwich is held together by a grid of knots stitched through all three layers. The thread for this needs to be thicker: pearl cotton is good or double knitting wool for a rustic effect – details are given with individual quilt instructions. A sharp needle with a large eye is essential. Use a long length of thread to allow for multiple tying.

1 Starting in the center of the place where you wish to position the tie, take a stitch through all three layers, draw the thread through, leaving a tail about 6 in/15 cm long. Reenter the quilt at the point where the next tie is to be and take another stitch, leaving a loop between stitches.

2 Repeat, without cutting, until there is a stitch in each of the places to have a tie (shown below).

3 Cut between the stitches, then tie the threads using a surgeon's square knot (shown below).

BINDING THE QUILT

If the quilt has been bagged out, it will not need a binding. Otherwise, after quilting, trim the edges so that all three layers are level. The binding is best done with doublefold binding, which can be cut either straight or on the bias. This can be made from straight strips joined together or as a continuous bias strip.

Continuous strip bias binding

1 Cut a square and mark the edges **A**, **B**, **C**, and **D**; cut through the diagonal (diagram 1), then stitch **A** to **B** with a ¼ in/0.75 cm seam allowance (diagram 2).

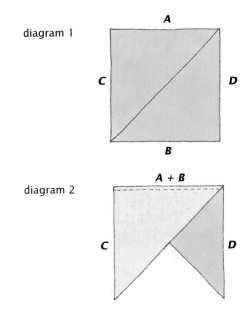

diagram 1

diagram 2

2 Open out and press the seam open. Draw lines the width of the bias you are making on the wrong side of the fabric (shown below).

3 Join **C** to **D**, right sides together, but dropping the seam by one strip and matching the marked lines. Pin and stitch the seam, then press open (shown below).

4 Cut the tube open along the marked lines in a continuous line (shown below).

Double-fold binding

1 Fold the fabric strip in half lengthwise, right side out, and press lightly.

2 Starting somewhere along one edge of the quilt, pin the binding to the quilt, leaving a tail (shown below).

3 Stitch, using ¼ in/0.75 cm seam allowance, until you are ¼ in/0.75 cm from the corner. Reverse stitch and break off the thread.

4 Fold the binding away from the quilt at a right angle (shown below, left), then fold it back down on itself, matching the edge of the binding with the edge of the quilt (shown below, right).

5 Starting ¼ in/0.75 cm from the corner, stitch to the next corner and repeat. Continue in this way until you are back where you started.

6 Fold back the two ends (shown below). Finger press, then stitch together along the creases. Trim back to ¼ in/0.75 cm.

7 Turn the binding over the edge to the back of the quilt, slipstitch down covering the machine stitches. At the corners, miters will fall on both front and back.

ADDING A HANGING SLEEVE

If your quilt is to be hung, either on the wall at home or in an exhibition, it will need a hanging sleeve.

1 Cut a piece of fabric 9 in/23 cm wide and equal to the width of the quilt. Turn a ½ in/1 cm hem at each short end and machine stitch.

2 Fold in half along its length, right sides together, and stitch the raw edges together with a ½ in/1 cm seam. Turn right sides out and press so that the seam is in the middle. You can adjust the pressing of the sleeve at this point so that the front of the sleeve is deeper than the back. When stitched to the quilt, the sleeve will have a slight bulge which will accommodate the thickness of the hanging pole.

3 Slipstitch the sleeve to the back of the quilt along the sleeve's top and bottom edges, placing the top edge just below the binding and making sure that the seam side is underneath.

LABELING A QUILT

It is important to sign and date your quilt as a record for yourself and future generations. The label you stitch onto your quilt can be simple or elaborate. There are books of scrolls that you can trace onto a simple calico label with a fine permanent pen. You can iron freezer paper to the wrong side of the label and type the details on the fabric. Remove the freezer paper before stitching the label to the reverse of the quilt.

ZIGZAGS and MEANDERS

The first two of my country quilts are based on ancient patterns, adapted to be made from appliqué or strips, then laid out in a quite formal "strip style." The next three quilts are made from the same combination of strip widths in twists on traditional patterns, so that two come out with zigzags and another as a large weave. The sixth quilt is an unusual star pattern. I can imagine them as a splash of cheerful color on a brass or solid wood bedstead in a white-washed beamed attic bedroom.

My fabrics for the first five are not scraps, because working with these usually takes longer. Like me, you will probably find that the choice of one fabric leads inevitably in a certain direction to the second and third – sometimes with unexpected results! For speed you need to use the rotary cutter and sewing machine. For relaxation, you might choose to hand piece (not me!) or hand quilt. Whatever methods you use, the initial choices of design and color will take just the same time. Why not take advantage of preplanning and try a ready-designed quilt?

– PAULINE ADAMS

GREEK KEY PATTERN

This ancient pattern, often found on early Greek pottery in black and terracotta,
is still a popular design motif in its many (some very complicated) variations. I originally designed this
for strip piecing but found an irresistible dress fabric that would have been hard to piece because of its stretchy weave
and linear pattern. So the design evolved into an appliqué pattern. It took approximately eight hours. This size of
quilt will make a jazzy topper for a single bed or an eye-catching sofa throw.

◆

Quilt size: 54 x 66 in/135 x 165 cm

MATERIALS

All fabrics used in the quilt top are 45 in/115 cm wide.

Black, fine-point, permanent marker pen
Tracing or waxed paper
Fusible webbing: 18 x 27 in/45.5 x 70 cm
Charcoal gray print fabric: 1¾ yards/1.6 meters
Cinnamon solid fabric: 1¾ yards/1.6 meters

Baking parchment paper
Cinnamon rayon machine-embroidery thread
Cardboard
Batting: 2 oz polyester, 70 x 58 in/175 x 145 cm
Backing: cotton or sheeting, 70 x 58 in/175 x 145 cm
Clear nylon machine-quilting thread

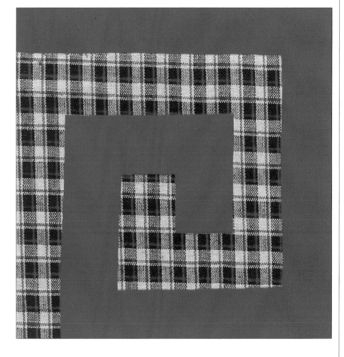

ALTERNATIVE COLOR SCHEMES

Although this pattern uses only two fabrics, it can look completely different, depending on which colors you choose to work with. Clockwise from top left: indigo and calico still provide a strong contrast but are more rural and folksy; blue and green prints produce a subtle and feminine look; splashy roses for the darker shade with a toning pastel pink look romantic and cottagey; and a homespun check with a strong contrast solid makes a very popular combination.

❝When choosing large-scale prints to use in large areas, as in this pattern, be sure to preview a good expanse of the fabric to ensure its suitability.❞

CUTTING

1 Draw the cutting pattern (shown below) for the key appliqué pieces, using the lines on your cutting mat as a guide, a rotary ruler, and permanent marker pen to enlarge the diagram, onto waxed or tracing paper. Lay the fusible webbing on top of the pattern (paper side up) and trace the pattern twice onto the paper backing.

2 From the charcoal print, cut lengthwise pieces (shown below). Cut one **A** strip, 28½ x 56½ in/71.5 x 141.5 cm; one **C** strip, 5 ½ in x 56½ in/14 x 141.5 cm; and one full-length strip 5½ in/14 cm wide, subcut into one **D** strip, 28½ in/71.5 cm long; one **E** strip, 16½ in/41.5 cm long and two **F** squares, 5½ in/14 cm.

3 From the cinnamon plain fabric, cut lengthwise pieces (shown below). Cut one **B** strip, 16½ x 56½ in/41.5 x 141.5 cm; one **C**, one **D** and one **E** strip, and two **F** squares as for the charcoal print.

4 Following manufacturer's instructions with fusible webbing, iron the drawn patterns to the wrong side of the remaining cinnamon fabric, ensuring lines are on grain. Use baking parchment paper between fusible webbing and iron to protect the surfaces.

5 Carefully cut (with scissors) along all the drawn lines. Discard the four very narrow slivers, and you will have four square-spiral key pieces.

STITCHING

All seam allowances are a scant ¼ in/0.75 cm.

1 Using the quilt plan, lay the key pieces in place along the right side of charcoal piece **A**, noting that the top key is spaced a seam's width from the top edge, and all the rest 2 in/5 cm apart. The tails are all flush with the long raw side edge of **A**. Adjust positions before peeling off the protective paper backing from one key, replacing it and ironing it in position, using the baking parchment paper for protection again. Repeat with the remaining three shapes.

2 With cinnamon thread, stitch the key shapes down, close to their edges. This stitching will be hidden later.

3 Pin and stitch **A** to **B**, catching the ends of the key shapes into the seam.

ADDING THE BORDERS

1 Pin the long borders, **C**, to the sides of the quilt top. Press all seams toward charcoal fabric.

2 Pin and stitch small strips **D** to **E**, short ends together, and repeat, reversing the color sequence (see quilt plan) to make two short border strips. Add a small **F** square on either end, then pin and stitch these to the top and bottom of the quilt, matching seam lines. Press all seams toward charcoal fabric.

FINISHING THE QUILT

1 Paste the paper key pattern onto cardboard. Cut out the spirals. Place the patterns in position on the quilt top (shown below) and mark around them with a fabric marker. Note that tails of the pattern do not reach the appliqué – just extend lines with a ruler. Repeat down the length of the quilt.

2 Lay out the batting. Place the patchwork centered on top, right side up, and safety-pin the layers together.

3 With cinnamon embroidery thread through the machine needle, loosen thread tension slightly, and set machine for a wide zigzag, with a very short stitch length. Practice first on some spare fabric and batting. Zigzag the quilt all around the key shapes, just covering their raw edges. If you want consistency, zigzag all around the other cinnamon pieces also, but not around any outside edges.

4 Trim the batting to the size of the quilt top. Lay out the backing, right side up, and center the quilt top on it, right sides together. Pin around the edges, and stitch all around ¼ in/ 0.75 cm from the edge, leaving an opening large enough to turn the quilt through.

5 Trim the corners and excess backing. Turn through and stitch the opening closed by hand. Safety-pin again through all layers.

6 With clear nylon thread through the needle, machine quilt on all seamlines and on the marked key shapes.

> ❝When quilting the key shapes, stitch all the lengthwise lines first, then the crosswise ones, rather than trying to quilt a continuous line round all the key corners.❞

BLUE MEANDERS

This is another ancient, very graphic pattern. Here I have set it in an unorthodox way as a stripe,
running from top to bottom, for a single-bed quilt. It took roughly twenty hours.

Quilt size: 62 x 94 in/155 x 235 cm

MATERIALS

All fabrics used in the quilt top are 45 in/115 cm wide.

White fabric: 4 yards/3.7 meters
Dark blue print fabric: 1½ yards/1.4 meters

Backing: cotton or sheeting, 70 x 99 in /178 x 250 cm
Batting: 2 oz polyester, a single-bed-sized piece
Quilting thread: 2 skeins blue pearl cotton no. 5
(optional)

CUTTING

1 Refer to the quilt plan and from the white fabric, cut (lengthwise) three background **A** strips 10½ in x 94 in/ 26.5 x 235 cm long, two **D** strips 2½ in x 94 in/6.5 x 235 cm and two **C** strips 2½ x 58 in/6.5 x 146.5 cm. Reserve for trimming to length later.

2 From the remaining white fabric, cut 11 crosswise strips, 2½ in/6.5 cm wide.

3 From the blue fabric, cut two crosswise strips, 6½ in/ 16.5 cm wide and 26 crosswise strips 2½ in/6.5 cm wide. Reserve 15 of the smaller strips for the borders.

STITCHING

The blue and white strips must be stitched into three different strip arrangements, as shown below, before pressing and cutting pattern units. Press all the strips toward the blue fabric.

4½ in/11.5 cm

unit a

10½ in/26.5 cm

unit b

2½ in/6.5 cm

unit c

6½ in/16.5 cm

unit d

4½ in/11.5 cm

unit e

2½ in/6.5 cm

unit f

1 For **a** units, you will need two lengths of two narrow blue strips stitched to one narrow white strip. Cut across into 18 pieces of 4½ in/11.5 cm.

2 For **c** units, you will need two lengths of one narrow white strip stitched to one 6½ in/16.5 cm wide blue strip. Cut across into 20 pieces, each 2½ in/6.5 cm wide.

3 For the remaining units you will need eight lengths of one narrow white strip stitched to one narrow blue strip. From these, first cut 18 **b** units, 10½ in/26.5 cm long. Next cut four **d** units 6½ in/16.5 cm long; four **e** units 4½ in/11.5 cm long and two white **f** units, 2½ in/6.5 cm square. (For the latter, undo a seam from the leftover joined strips if necessary.)

4 Divide the units into two equal piles and work first with one of them. Following diagram 2 on page 26, start at the top of the left-hand strip and work downward. Stitch the top **d** unit to an **a** unit, adding alternate **b** and **a** units until you have used five **a** units; finish with the second **d** unit.

5 For the middle strip, stitch 10 **c** units end to end and finish with a white **f** square.

6 For the right-hand strip, start at the top with an **e** unit stitched to a **b** unit, then alternate **a** and **b** units until all in the first pile have been used up, finishing with the final **e** unit.

7 Press all the strips, then pin and stitch the lengths together as shown on page 26, right. Press again. Make the second patchwork strip exactly the same.

ASSEMBLY AND BORDERS

1 Stitch the reserved blue strips into one long length. Press the seams open. Measure the length of the patchwork pattern strips and cut the three reserved wide white background pieces (**A**) to this length.

2 Cut two lengths off the blue stripping to the same measurement (border strips **B**).

3 For border strips **D**, cut two lengths of blue stripping and two of white all 8 in/20 cm longer than **A** and **B**. Reserve.

4 Assemble the top, including borders **B**, noting that the right-hand patchwork strip must be turned end to end to mirror the left-hand strip. Pin, stitch, and press all long seams.

5 Measure across the patchwork center side to center side; cut two white and two blue **C** border strips to this length, and two blue **E** border strips 8 in/20 cm longer. Pin and stitch blue and white pairs of border strips together. Press the seams toward the blue borders.

6 Pin and stitch the border strips to the patchwork, first **C** strips to top and bottom, then **D** strips to each side, and finally **E** strips to top and bottom. Press the seams toward the blue fabric between additions.

FINISHING THE QUILT

1 Using the patchwork as a guide, lightly mark the horizontal lines for the rectangles in the plain strips, then mark the vertical lines, which are 2 in/5 cm apart.

2 Layer the backing, batting and patchwork. Safety-pin through all the layers.

3 Machine quilt in the ditch around the patchwork patterns and on all the border seams (except the crosswise joining seams). Machine quilt in the white background strips or sashiko quilt the pattern, using pearl cotton in a matching blue.

4 Trim the batting ¼ in/0.75 cm smaller than the quilt top. Trim the backing to the same size as the quilt top. Fold the backing over to enclose the batting and turn the top in to match, both with ¼ in/0.75 cm turnings. Pin and machine stitch all around, close to the edge.

RAIL FENCE VARIATION

This quilt pattern is based on the traditional American pattern Rail Fence, but I have changed the strips from equal to varied width and changed the set of the patchwork blocks to on point. Using one wide strip eliminates seams and so is quicker. These changes result in an unusual zigzag design. The fabrics chosen are strong and bright. The wider print strip counterbalances the narrower blue. It took about twelve hours to make, and is sized for a child's bed, a throw, a lap quilt, or a topper for a double bed.

◆

Quilt size: 57 x 57 in / 143 x 143 cm

MATERIALS

All fabrics used in the quilt top are 45 in/115 cm wide.

Printed fabric for wide strips and outer border: 2 yards/1.9 meters
White (or light) solid fabric for narrow strips: ⅞ yard/80 cm

Dark solid fabric for narrow strips and inner border: 1¼ yards/1.1 meters
Cardboard
Backing: cotton or sheeting, 60 in/155 cm square
Batting: 2 oz polyester, 60 in/155 cm square
Knitting worsted

CUTTING

1 From the printed fabric, cut 14 crosswise strips, 4½ in/ 11.5 cm wide. Reserve six for the outer border.

2 From the white fabric, cut eight crosswise strips, 2½ in/ 6.5 cm wide.

3 From the dark solid fabric, cut 13 crosswise strips, 2½ in/6.5 cm wide. Reserve five for the inner border.

STITCHING

1 Stitch one strip of each color into eight sets of three using a scant ¼ in/0.75 cm seam allowance. Press the seams toward the print fabric (shown below).

2 Measure across the stripping and cut it into 24 squares of that measurement. This is most easily done with a large square rotary ruler, but may also be done with a cardboard template cut to the right size and laid as a guide under an ordinary rotary ruler.

3 Make a triangular cardboard template, with the short sides ³⁄₈ in/1.125 cm longer than the side of the squares you have just cut.

4 Cut 16 half blocks for the quilt edges from the remaining stripping (shown below), noting that each half-block triangle will have one point missing. Pin and stitch the blocks and half blocks in diagonal rows (shown top, right). Finger press the seams.

5 Stitch the rows together into a square. Finger press the seams. Tame the seam crossings. Press carefully with the grain so as not to distort the bias edges.

ADDING THE BORDERS

1 Stitch the five reserved dark plain fabric strips for the inner border into one long length. Press the seams open.

2 Measure the patchwork across the center. Cut two dark strips to this length and two strips 4 in/10 cm longer. Following the quilt plan, pin and stitch the two shorter borders to the opposite sides of the patchwork, then the two longer strips to the remaining sides. Press the seams outward.

3 Stitch the six reserved printed fabric strips for the outer border into one long length. Press. Measure the patchwork across the center again. Cut two print strips to this length and two strips 8 in/20 cm longer. Pin and stitch the two shorter borders to opposite sides of the patchwork. Press. Stitch the two longer strips to the remaining sides. Press.

FINISHING THE QUILT

The quilt is machine quilted in two stages before and after being bagged out.

1 Cut the backing and batting 4 in/10 cm larger in each direction than the quilt top.

2 Lay out the batting. Place the quilt top right side up on top of it. Safety-pin the layers together at the center of each block, along the middle of the print border and in the triangular edge blocks.

3 Machine quilt in the ditch on the long edges of all the white plain strips, and between the two border strips. If desired, also quilt along the center of all the print strips in the blocks. Trim off any excess batting.

4 Leaving the pins in, lay out the patchwork right side up. Lay the backing on top, right side down. Pin. Stitch around ¼ in/0.75 cm from the patchwork edge, but leave an opening about 12 in/30 cm long for turning the quilt through. Trim any excess backing and snip off the corners. Turn through. Stitch the opening closed by hand.

5 Safety-pin again through all layers. Machine quilt in the ditch around the individual blocks, the inner border seam, and ½ in/1.5 cm from the outside edge.

6 If desired, tie through all the layers on the print strips and borders. The positions are marked on the quilt plan. Use knitting worsted, doubled, and a large-eyed sharp needle. A quick, economical knot is shown below. To do this, take a stitch through all layers, pull yarn through, leaving a 2 in/5.5 cm tail on top. Flip the yarn in a loop around the far side of the tail, then take hold of the tail with one hand while passing the needle up through the front of the loop with the other. Pull firmly on the needle and tail to tie the knot close to the quilt's surface. Trim off the ends to 1 in/2.5 cm.

WEAVE PATTERN

The same set of one wide and two narrow strips can be used in many different ways by changing the colors, the strip sequence, and/or the arrangement of blocks. Here the strips have been arranged differently, and the blocks are in two different color patterns, so that the overall effect is of a piece of weaving. Instead of machine quilting down the center strips, try equally speedy tying or leisurely hand quilting. The solid colors chosen are of equal strength to emphasize the pattern. This project took roughly eleven hours and makes a pretty lap or child's quilt.

✦

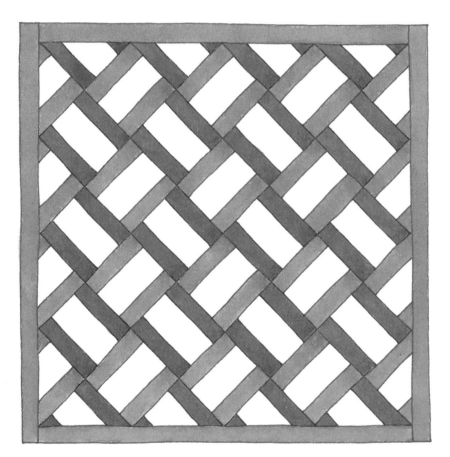

Quilt size: 49¼ x 49¼ in/123 x 123 cm

MATERIALS

All fabrics used in the quilt top are 45 in/115 cm wide.

Pink cotton fabric: 1¼ yards/1.2 meters
Blue cotton fabric: 1 yard/90 cm
White cotton fabric: 1½ yards/1.4 meters

Cardboard: about 10 in/25 cm square
Batting: 2 oz polyester, 54 in/140 cm square
Clear nylon machine-quilting thread
Backing: cotton or sheeting, 54 in/140 cm square

CUTTING

1 From the pink fabric, cut 15 crosswise strips, 2½ in/6.5 cm wide. Reserve five for the border.

2 From the blue fabric, cut 10 crosswise strips, 2½ in/6.5 cm wide.

3 From the white fabric, cut 10 crosswise strips, 4½ in/ 11.5 cm wide.

STITCHING

Use a scant ¼ in/0.75 cm seam allowance throughout.

1 Stitch one strip of each color into ten sets of three – five with blue strips on either side of the white and five with pink strips on either side of the white (shown below). Press the seams away from the white fabric.

2 Measure across a pressed strip set. Cut 12 squares of each color pattern of stripping to this measurement.

3 Cut a right-angle triangle template from the cardboard, with short sides ½ in/1.25 cm longer than the measured stripping width. From the remaining stripping, cut eight triangle blocks of each color pattern (shown below). Note that each half-block triangle will have one point missing.

4 Following the quilt plan, lay out the blocks in pattern. Pin and stitch them together in diagonal strips (shown top, right). Press carefully so as not to distort the bias edges.

ADDING THE BORDERS

1 Stitch the reserved pink strips for the border into one long length. Press the seams open.

2 Measure across the center of the quilt top. Cut two pieces to this measurement and two pieces 4 in/10 cm longer.

3 Pin on, then stitch the two shorter borders to opposite sides of the quilt top. Pin, then stitch the longer borders to the other two sides. Press.

FINISHING THE QUILT

The quilt is partly machine quilted before being bagged out, then machine quilted again.

1 Mark a line for quilting down the center of all the blocks, through the length of the white strips.

2 Lay out the batting. Lay the quilt top on top of the batting, right side up and safety-pin the layers together.

3 Using nylon quilting thread through the machine needle and with a slightly lengthened stitch, machine quilt in the ditch on the long edges of all the white strips and on the marked lines. Trim the batting to the size of the quilt top.

4 Lay out the backing, right side up. Lay the quilt top centered on top of the backing, right side down. Pin around the edges. Stitch around the edge, ¼ in/0.75 cm in from the quilt edge, leaving an opening for turning. Trim the corners. Turn through and stitch the opening closed by hand.

5 Safety-pin again. Machine quilt ½ in/1.5 cm from the quilt edge, then in the ditch of the borders; finally, machine quilt in long diagonal lines across the quilt on all the block edges.

PUSS-IN-LIGHTNING

The traditional strip quilt layout has wide alternate-colored strips of fabric running the length of the quilt. I have used the Puss in the Corner block on point in vertical rows but eliminated strip seams by setting it staggered and diagonally, like the pattern Streak of Lightning – less stitching and more effect! The finish is machine quilting, but you could embellish with ties or buttons. There will be one spare block, which could be used for a matching pillow. This size of quilt is suitable for a lap quilt or a throw and took about twelve hours.

◆

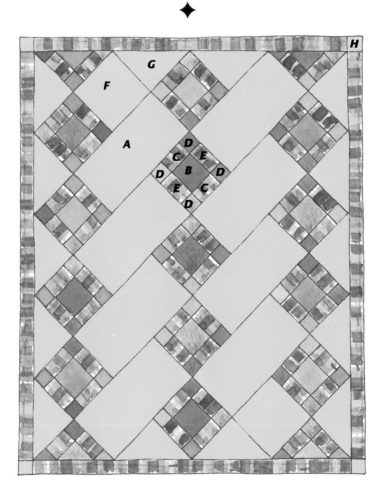

Quilt size: 49¼ x 60½ in/123 x 154.5 cm

MATERIALS

All fabrics used in the quilt top are 45 in/115 cm wide.

Background fabric: solid color, 1¾ yards/1.5 meters
Solid fabric: six fat quarters in assorted colors (there will be left-overs)

Plaid fabric: 1½ yards/1.3 meters
Batting: 2 oz polyester, 65 in x 53 in/162 x 133 cm
Clear nylon machine-quilting thread
Backing: light-colored cotton or sheeting, 65 in x 53 in/162 x 133 cm

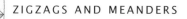
CUTTING

1 From the background fabric, cut four crosswise strips 8½ in/21.5 cm wide, then cut these into eight **A** pieces 16½ in/41.75 cm long and two **F** squares (see quilt plan).

2 From the same fabric, cut two crosswise strips 9 in/23 cm wide, and cut into seven squares. Cut these in half diagonally to make 14 **G** triangles.

3 From the background remnants, cut four **H** pieces 2½ in/ 5.5 cm square.

4 From the plaid fabric, cut six crosswise strips 4½ in/ 11.5 cm wide, then cut in half. Cut 11 crosswise strips 2½ in/ 6.5 cm wide; cut six of these in half and reserve the remaining five for the borders.

5 From each fat quarter, cutting at right angles to the selvage, cut one strip 4½ in/11.5 cm wide and two strips 2½ in/6.5 cm wide.

STITCHING

All seams are a scant ¼ in/0.75 cm. For the blocks, the plaid and solid fabric strips are stitched into sets of three, then recut and stitched into squares.

1 For the **B** and **C** pieces, start by stitching a narrow plaid strip to each long side of a wide fat quarter strip; press seam allowances toward the plaid; trim the ends even and cut each of the six sets across into three lengths of 4½ in/11.5 cm (shown below).

2 For **D** and **E** pieces, stitch one narrow fat quarter strip to each long side of a wide plaid strip, making sure that the solids are different colors. Stitch into six sets; press the seams toward the plaid, trim the ends, then cut across into six pieces 2½ in/ 6.5 cm wide (shown above, left).

3 Lay out all these pieces to form 18 blocks, making sure that each block contains five differently colored solids (shown above, right). Pin and stitch the pieces into blocks and press.

4 Lay out the quilt top as shown below. Note that there will be one spare block, and that the four blocks sticking out at top and bottom will be trimmed later. Pin and stitch each row separately. Finger press the seams away from the blocks.

5 Pin and stitch the diagonal rows together. Press carefully with the grain so as not to distort the bias edges.

6 Using a rotary ruler, mark a line ¼ in/0.75 cm outside the block corners at the quilt top edges. Trim on this line.

ADDING THE BORDERS

1 For the border, stitch the reserved plaid strips together into one long length. Press the seams open.

2 Measure the quilt top width and length, across the center. Cut two border strips to the measured width and two to the measured length. Pin on and stitch the short borders to the top and bottom of the quilt. Finger press at the ends. Stitch one **H** square to each end of the two long border strips. Pin and stitch these strips to opposite sides. Press.

FINISHING THE QUILT

The quilt is machine quilted in two stages – before and after bagging out.

1 Mark the quilt top for quilting: using the rotary ruler, mark parallel zigzag lines to the blocks on the background fabric, spaced 2 in/5 cm away from them, with a third line halfway between.

2 Lay out the batting smoothly, and place the quilt top on top, right side up, ensuring that the batting is larger on all sides than the top. Safety-pin in all the block squares, along the border, and on the background.

3 Machine quilt with a lengthened stitch and clear nylon quilting thread. First stitch on all the marked zigzag lines, then in the ditch of the internal seamlines of the blocks.

4 Trim the excess batting, so that it is the same size as the quilt top. Lay out the backing, right side up and lay the quilt top onto it, right side down. Pin all round, then stitch ¼ in/0.75 cm inside the edge of the quilt top, leaving an opening on one side large enough to turn the quilt through. Trim off the excess backing and clip the corners. Turn through.

5 Fold in and pin the seam allowances of the opening and hand hem. Safety-pin again along the border and on all small corner squares of the blocks. Machine quilt ¼ in/0.75 cm from outside edge and in the ditch of the border and the block edges.

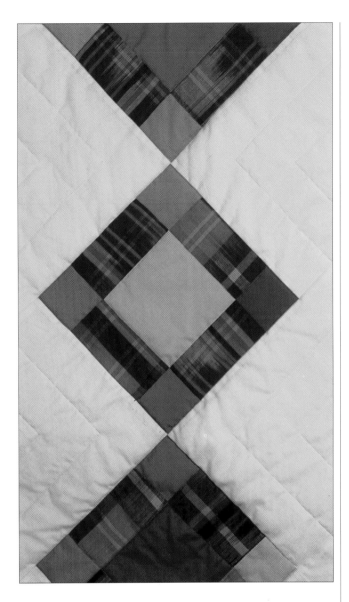

❝ The use of a walking or even-feed foot is very helpful when machine quilting. It feeds top and bottom fabrics through the machine evenly. ❞

STAR GAZING

This pattern gets its name from the stars formed by the stripped sections of the blocks.
Traditional American pattern names are Mountain Star and Stars and Stripes. Here, the units are arranged
in different combinations to form two star shapes.

◆

Quilt size: 54½ x 54½ in/136.5 x 136.5 cm

MATERIALS

All fabrics used in the quilt top are 45 in/115 cm wide.

Cardboard or template plastic
Border fabric and square for wedges: solid cotton fabric, 3 yards/2.7 meters

Spray starch
Stripping: printed cotton fabric, 9 assorted fat quarters
Backing: cotton or sheeting, 60 x 60 in/ 1.5 x 1.5 meters
Batting: 2 oz polyester, 60 x 60 in/1.5 x 1.5 meters

There are three different star formations in this quilt. I made it using pink poplin and floral cotton lawn scraps from my fabric hoard for the stripping, but the instructions assume new fabrics will be used. It can be made two ways. I made it by stitching the strips in turn onto a paper foundation square to which the central wedge had been pinned. A quicker way (taking about 14 hours) is to make stripping and stitch triangles of it onto the top of a square, then trim off the excess, which removes the tedious and messy stage of picking off the paper backing. The size of the quilt makes it suitable for a baby's crib or a lap quilt. You could try bright and zingy colors as an alternative to the pastels.

CUTTING

1 Cut a wedge-shaped template from cardboard or template plastic using the pattern on page 45.

2 From the border/wedge fabric, cut the borders: two lengthwise strips, 3½ in/9 cm wide and 60 in/153 cm long, and two more the same width but 66 in/168 cm long. These measurements are overlong to allow for variations in the finished size.

3 Spray-starch and press the remaining border/wedge fabric. From it cut sixty-four 6½ in/16.5 cm squares. Place the wedge template on the right side of each square and mark both diagonal lines (shown below).

4 Divide the fat quarters for the stripping into three sets of three. Lay one set of three on the cutting mat. Trim the short sides and cut 1½ in/4 cm wide strips parallel to the short side, cutting a total of 11 strips. Repeat with the remaining two sets of three. There will be some remnants to use up on another project or in case of accidents.

STITCHING

1 Stitch the strips together down the long sides in sets of three, varying the color schemes as much as possible and using a scant ¼ in/0.75 cm seam allowance. Press the seams to one side, then spray-starch and press again.

2 Trim across the end of each piece of stripping and cut across into two 8½ in/21.5 cm rectangles. Cut each rectangle in half diagonally. If you want your fabrics to be symmetrically placed around each wedge, be sure to cut the second rectangle of each set of stripping with the diagonal in the other direction (shown below). Cut 64 rectangles altogether.

3 Pin and stitch a stripping triangle to a square, with the straight edge of the strip against the marked line (shown on page 43). Remember to stitch with a scant seam allowance. Finger press the stripping triangle outward. Stitch a (matching) mirror-image triangle to the other side. Press, spray-starch, and press again. It will be a strange shape until it is finally trimmed in step 4. Repeat step 3 until all the squares have had stripping triangles stitched to them.

4 Lay each pieced unit on the cutting mat, wrong side up. Use the square's edges as a guide to trim off excess stripping to make the unit 6½ in/16.5 cm square. Finally trim off the corner flaps of the square where they lie on the wrong side of the stripping.

5 Place a large sheet on the floor and arrange the pieced units in sets of four to make stars (see quilt plan). Pin to the sheet to ensure that the arrangement does not get muddled. Remove the units from the sheet when you are ready to stitch them together, first into rows (finger press seams open), then stitch the rows together (still finger pressing the seams). Do not press with an iron until the borders are stitched on, otherwise all the bias edges will distort.

ADDING THE BORDERS

1 For the top and bottom borders, measure across the center of the pieced top, center side to center side. Cut two border strips to this measurement. Pin on and stitch.

2 For the side borders, measure across the quilt, center top to center bottom and cut the remaining two border strips to fit. Pin them on and stitch. Press.

FINISHING THE QUILT

The quilt is bagged out, then machine quilted. You could tie it for a quicker finish or hand quilt it at your leisure.

1 Cut the backing exactly the same size as the completed quilt top and the batting 4 in/10 cm larger in each direction.

2 Mark the quilt top for quilting, if desired.

3 Lay the batting out smoothly. Lay the pieced top over the batting, right sides up, with the excess batting extending evenly on all sides. Safety-pin the layers together. Lay the backing over the pieced top, right sides together and matching edges. Pin all around the edge. Turn over and trim the batting evenly with the quilt top.

4 Stitch all around the quilt, ¼ in/0.75 cm in from the fabric edge but leave an opening of 8 in/20 cm in the center of one side. Snip off corner points before turning through.

5 Repin through all the layers. Hand stitch the opening closed. Machine stitch all around the quilt ¼ in/0.75 cm from the edge. If you are machine quilting, stitch around the kipper shapes, along all the block edges, and in the border seams. Otherwise, tie through all three layers.

““Take care not to stretch the bias edges of the quilt top when pinning and stitching the borders.””

STAR GAZING PATTERN

CHANGING SEASONS

The sewing machine, modern tools, and the rotary cutter have revolutionized quiltmaking today; however, for me it is still important that we do not lose sight of the humble origins of the craft, and this underlies my choice of fabrics and designs for the quilts in this chapter. I have incorporated modern techniques with traditional skills at the same time using basic materials with simple block designs; I have taken a look at the ways in which these were used in the early days of quiltmaking.

Ideas for the quilt designs came mainly from old quilts; I took my color inspiration from the countryside where I live and the ever-changing seasons.

– GILL TURLEY

FALL COLORS

All the colors of autumn are contained in this lap quilt, ranging from the subtle greens,
burnished gold, and bronze to the muted browns. Soft, brushed-cotton fabrics, reminiscent of laborers'
shirts of the past, are pieced to make the simple Courthouse Steps variation of the traditional Log Cabin block.
It took about twenty-four hours. An interesting dimension is added to the overall design of this quilt by placing
a large plaid square between each log cabin block, which also speeds up the piecing. Utility quilting
and buttons, of both leather and wood, add the final touches.

◆

Quilt size: 59½ x 59½ in/151 x 151 cm

MATERIALS

All fabrics used in the quilt are 45 in/115 cm wide.

Small check fabric for the Courthouse Steps blocks:
green, 50 in/125 cm; light gold, 40 in/100 cm
**Large check fabric for Courthouse Steps small
center squares:** dark green, 8 in/20 cm square
Large check fabric for large squares: dark green,
36 in/90 cm; light gold, 12 in/30 cm
Border blocks: dark brown small check, 20 x 45 in/
50 x 115 cm

Corner squares for border: light brown small print,
12 in/15 cm square
Backing: 62 in/158 cm square
Batting: cotton, 62 in/158 cm square
Quilting thread: embroidery thread
Buttons: 12 assorted leather and wood buttons for tying
Binding: 24 in/60 cm square

ALTERNATIVE COLOR SCHEMES

Different combinations of fabrics produce very different effects, particularly changing the relationship between the strips and the large squares. I have chosen four variations still with the country theme in mind. Dark stars on a creamy background with clover pink produces a fresh look (top left); dramatic stripes make a strong accent amid soft purples and beiges (top right); mossy greens and watery blues create an air of tranquility (bottom left); while muted browns and blues combined with sand colors suggest fallow fields in winter (bottom right).

COURTHOUSE STEPS BLOCKS
Cutting

1 Work on the small check fabrics for the strips and the large check for the small center squares. From the green small check, cut one strip 5 x 26 in/13.5 x 66 cm (**A**). Reserve to use when making the half blocks for the border.

2 To cut the rest of the strips, place the green and light gold small check fabrics together. Cut across the full width of the fabric, cutting strips 2 in/5.5 cm wide.

3 From the dark green large check, cut twelve 2 in/5.5 cm squares for the centers of the blocks.

Stitching

1 Place a strip of light gold check fabric under the machine foot and position the first center square on top, right sides together. Line up the raw edges, then chain piece, adding the squares until all 12 squares have been stitched. Press the seam toward the strip, then trim the units apart (shown below).

2 Stitch another light gold strip to the opposite side of the squares (shown top, right). Press and trim as before.

3 Chain piece the green strips to the remaining two sides in the same way. Press and trim as before.

4 Continue adding the light gold and green rows until there are three rows on each side of the small squares. The 12 pieced blocks should each measure 11 in/33 cm square. However, if you are using loosely woven cottons, these may be more stretchy, which could cause a discrepancy in size.

LARGE SQUARE BLOCKS
Cutting

1 Measure the 12 Courthouse Steps blocks and check that they are all the same size. Use this measurement to cut the large squares.

2 Cut out the large squares from the large check fabric. Cut four from the light gold and nine from the dark green. If the measurements are accurate, these will be cut as 11 in/33 cm squares. If your pieced blocks vary from the given measurement, then cut your large squares to match the size of your pieced blocks. Note that you will also need to adapt the measurements when making the half blocks for the border.

Stitching

1 Machine stitch the large squares to the Courthouse Steps blocks in rows (shown below), then join the rows together as in the sequence shown in the quilt plan. Press the seams toward the large squares.

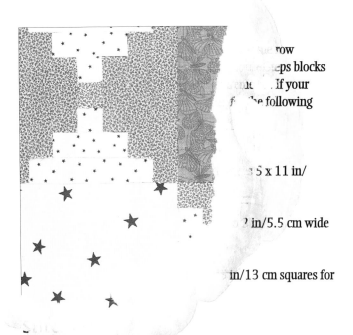

row

ps blocks

If your

the following

5 x 11 in/

2 in/5.5 cm wide

in/13 cm squares for

1 To make   ks, machine stitch the dark brown **C** strips to each o   e   ng edges of the reserved green small check **A** piece. Press seams toward the dark brown strips.

2 Subcut every 2 in/5.5 cm to make the beginnings of the pieced half blocks, a total of 12 units (shown below).

3 Stitch a long strip of green small check to one long side of these units. Press and trim.

4 Add dark brown **C** strips to each short side of the units. Press and trim.

5 Add one more green small check strip (shown above, right) to complete the half blocks.

6 Alternating the blocks, join the half blocks to the **B** pieces to make the four borders. To complete the top and bottom borders stitch a corner square to each end as in the quilt plan.

7 Stitch the short borders to opposite sides of the quilt top. Press the seams toward the borders.

8 Stitch the top and bottom borders to the remaining two edges of the quilt. Press the seams toward the borders.

FINISHING THE QUILT

1 Prepare the quilt for quilting. Layer the backing, batting, and quilt top. Baste the layers together.

2 Use thick thread and utility quilting (see page 62) to stitch diagonal lines from corner to corner on the plain blocks. In the center of each pieced block, stitch a button. To finish, make a double bias binding and bind the quilt.

STRING PATCHWORK DIAMONDS

The fresh colors of the string diamonds of this single-bed quilt remind me of spring.
They are made from shirting samples and are machine stitched onto diamond-shaped muslin foundation pieces.
The striped fabrics used for the strings give a fan effect, achieved by stitching the strings at a slight angle, fanning from
the center outward. A plain diamond is used to offset each string diamond. The quilt is finished with hand quilting,
but for speed it could be machine quilted or tied, in which case it will take about thirty hours.

◆

Quilt size: 58 x 54 in/148 x 138 cm

MATERIALS

All fabrics used in the quilt top are 45 in/115 cm wide.

Thin cardboard or template plastic
For foundation diamonds: muslin, 39 in/100 cm
For string diamonds: plenty of strips of scrap fabrics or
5 different striped and plaid fabrics, 12 in/30 cm of each

For plain diamonds: 39 in/100 cm
Border fabric: 39 in/100 cm
Corner squares fabric: 10 in/25 cm
Batting: 60 x 72 in/152 x 183 cm
Backing: 60 x 72 in/152 x 183 cm
Binding: 24 in/60 cm square

String piecing is a popular way of making a quilt, either to recycle good pieces of cloth salvaged from old clothing or to use up odd pieces left over from dressmaking; these scraps were sometimes known as "strings." This method, which was formerly hand sewn with a running stitch, was originally known as "pick-up work." The bag of strings could be stored in readiness, the foundation shapes cut out, and the work picked up and stitched, as and when time allowed. The diamond foundation shape can also be joined to make star blocks. Square and triangular foundations are popular, too, and used in other string patchwork designs.

CUTTING

1 Trace the diamond pattern provided on page 57 onto the template plastic or thin paper which can then be stuck onto cardboard. On your template mark the arrow to show the grain line, number each edge as shown, then cut out the template carefully. Note that seam allowances are included. (Use the width from your sewing machine needle to the edge of the presser foot as the seam guide for all seams.)

2 To cut the foundation diamonds, position the template on the top left-hand corner of the muslin, making sure that the arrow is in line with the straight grain of the fabric. Position the ruler on top of the template and along edge **1** of the diamond. Make the first cut using the full length of the ruler (shown at top). Before you move the ruler down to continue the cut, place a yard (meter) stick alongside, then carefully move the ruler along the edge of the stick and continue this first cut (shown middle). Using the template as a width guide, place the ruler on top of the cut strip and parallel to the line you have just cut, then cut again along edge **2** of the diamond (shown at bottom). Repeat this process, cutting long strips.

> **"** Use a piece of folded transparent tape to hold the template in position on the fabric. **"**

3 Layer the long rows carefully. Using the template as a guide, subcut the layered strips into diamonds using edges **3** (diagram 1) and **4** (diagram 2). You will need a total of 44 diamonds.

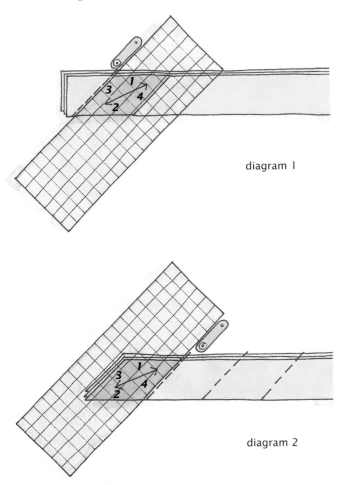

diagram 1

diagram 2

4 Cut the scrap fabrics for the string diamonds into manageable pieces, roughly 1–1½ in/2.5–4 cm wide and long enough to reach from the tip to the base of the diamond foundation.

5 To cut the plain fabric diamonds, cut long strips as described in step 2, using the diamond template and long ruler. Do not subcut into diamonds.

STITCHING
Stitching strings to foundation diamonds

1 Position the first string right side up on top of the muslin foundation (diagram 3). Take the next string, place it on top of the first string, right sides together, and move the bottom of this strip in a little, toward the center (diagram 4). Machine stitch and flip the second string open. Finger press if you are using crisp cottons, but if you are using wool or other fabrics, these may need to be pressed with a steam iron.

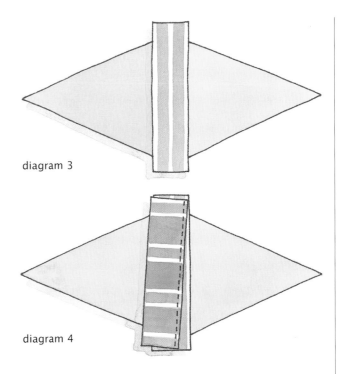

diagram 3

diagram 4

2 Continue stitching the strings in the same way to the left and right of the central strip, until the muslin foundation is completely covered.

3 Excess bulk can be removed by trimming spare fabric from the seam allowance. Do not trim the strips level with the edges of the foundation until you have pressed the completed diamond with the iron. To hold the last strings firmly in place, I recommend machine topstitching close to the edges of the diamond, at the narrow ends (shown below).

4 Press the completed diamond with the steam iron, turn the diamond over to the muslin side of the work, and trim strings even with the muslin edges (shown below). Make all the string diamonds in the same way.

Joining plain strips to string diamonds

1 Stitch the string diamonds to the long plain strips (diagram 1). Make sure that the grain line runs in the same direction on all pieces. When stitching has been completed, press the seams toward the plain strips, then cut the sections apart, as shown. This will produce pairs of one plain diamond and one string diamond.

2 Join pairs to make rows (diagram 2). The rows are joined diagonally across the quilt. Begin each row with a plain diamond and add one at the end of each row (you will need to cut some extra plain diamonds). These edge diamonds will be trimmed to size later.

3 Following the quilt plan, arrange the rows on the floor and number each with a label. Pick up the rows in sequence and machine stitch them together. Press the seams toward the bottom edge of the quilt. Trim away the excess fabric from the edge diamonds, making sure that you leave enough seam allowance on each side.

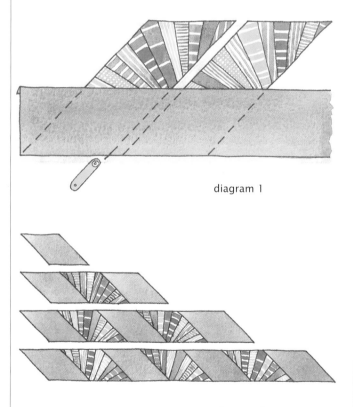

diagram 1

diagram 2

ADDING THE BORDERS

1 For the side borders, measure the quilt from the center top to center bottom. Cut two strips of border fabric to this length and 9½ in/24.5 cm wide.

2 For the top and bottom borders, measure across quilt, from center side to center side, before the side borders have been stitched to the quilt. Cut two strips to this measurement, 9½ in/24.5 cm wide.

3 For the corner squares, cut four 9½ in/24.5 cm squares. Stitch one square to each end of the top and bottom border strips. Press the seams toward the squares.

4 Stitch the side borders, then the top and bottom borders to the quilt top, matching centers. Press seams toward borders.

5 Layer the quilt top, batting, and backing and baste or pin together. Quilt if desired, or tie. I have quilted in the ditch round the diamonds and in a zigzag pattern in the border.

6 To finish the quilt make a 2 in/5 cm double bias binding using the continuous strip technique. Press the binding in half lengthwise. With right sides together, align the raw edges of the binding with the raw edges of the quilt. Using your machine presser foot as a seam guide (width from needle to foot edge), stitch the binding to the front of the quilt. Turn the binding over the raw edge and slipstitch the folded edge of binding to the back of the quilt.

STRING PATCHWORK
DIAMONDS PATTERN

DECORATIVE STITCHES SAMPLER

Make this simple Churn block patchwork and quilt it with a variety of decorative stitches. It could be used as either a crib quilt or a sampler to hang on the wall. The patchwork is quick to make on the sewing machine and the decorative stitches are easy and therapeutic to work by hand: the whole quilt took about thirty hours. These stitches produce a homespun look rather than a fine quilted effect and the colors are reminiscent of country-style winter clothing.

◆

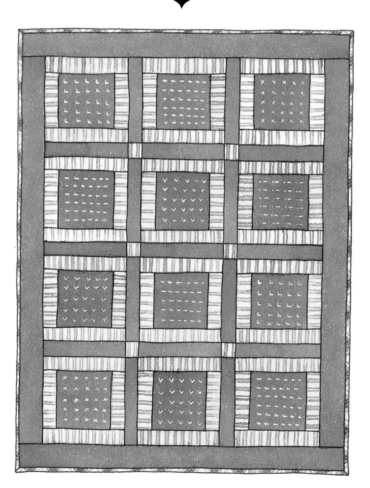

Quilt size: 35 x 45 in/89 x 114.5 cm

MATERIALS

All fabrics used in the quilt top are 45 in/115 cm wide.

Navy fabric: 1 yard/1 meter
Striped fabric: ¾ yard/70 cm
Backing: 40 x 48 in/100 x 120 cm
Batting: cotton, 40 x 48 in/100 x 120 cm

Quilting thread: embroidery thread in a contrasting color for the decorative stitches
Needles: assorted lengths with an eye large enough to take embroidery thread
Check binding fabric: 24 x 24 in/60 cm x 60cm

CUTTING

1 Using the navy fabric and cutting across the width, cut three strips (**A**) 6½ x 26 in/16.5 x 66 cm (as shown in the cutting plan below).

2 Subcut these bordered pieces every 6½ in/16.5 cm, to make 12 blocks (shown below).

3 From the remaining striped fabric strips, cut 24 shorter strips of 9½ in/24.5 cm. Stitch these borders to the sides of each of the 12 blocks (shown below). Press the seams toward the striped fabric.

2 Cut nine short strips (**B**) each 2 x 9½ in/5.5 x 24.5 cm. These are for joining the blocks.

3 From the remaining navy fabric and still cutting across the full width, cut two strips (**C**), 2 in/5.5 cm wide for joining the rows and four strips (**D**), 3 in/8 cm wide for the borders.

4 Using the striped fabric and cutting across the full width of the fabric across the stripes, cut thirteen 2 in/5.5 cm strips (**E**). These are for bordering the navy squares and for making the small striped squares that connect the completed blocks.

STITCHING

1 Take six of the 2 in/5.5 cm striped (**E**) strips and trim them so that they each measure 2 x 26 in/5.5 x 66 cm. Stitch to each of the long sides of the 6½ in/16.5 cm navy (**A**) strips (shown above, top right). Press the seams toward the striped fabric.

4 Using the scraps left over from the striped strips, cut six connecting squares, each 2 in/5.5 cm.

5 Take two of the navy 2 x 9½ in/5.5 x 24.5 cm (**B**) pieces and stitch them to join the first three blocks together to make the first row. Repeat, until you have completed four rows of three blocks (shown below). One short strip will be left over which will be used in the following step.

6 From the remaining 2 in/5.5 cm navy long (**C**) strips, cut eight more short strips each measuring 9½ in/24.5 cm. Join the short strips to the connecting squares, also using the strip left over from step 5 (shown below). When the strips are complete, join the four rows of blocks together with these strips in between. Press the seams toward the striped borders.

ADDING THE BORDERS

1 Measure the quilt top from top center to bottom center. From two of the 3 in/8 cm navy (**D**) strips, cut two borders to this measurement. Stitch these borders to each of the long sides of the quilt. Press the seams toward the center of the work.

2 For the top and bottom borders, measure across the quilt from side center edge to side center edge. Cut borders from the two remaining 3 in/8 cm navy (**D**) strips to this measurement. Stitch the top and bottom borders to the quilt and press the seams toward the striped borders.

FINISHING THE QUILT

1 Layer the backing, batting, and quilt top, then baste the layers together.

2 Work the decorative stitches described on page 62 using the embroidery thread and large-eyed needle. Place the work in a quilting hoop and begin by quilting the center blocks, then work out to the edges of the quilt. Following the stitch diagrams, work the different stitches creating two blocks of each stitch.

3 Some of the stitches are worked in rows from top to bottom and others are worked from right to left (opposite direction for left-handed stitchers). To start, knot one end of the thread and pop the knot through the top layer of fabric so that it remains hidden between the layers. To finish, make a knot close to the last stitch and pull the needle and thread between the layers. Bring the needle out a short distance away, then pop the knot through the top fabric and trim the thread. Make sure the end is hidden in the quilt layers. Note that the **B** to **C** stage of each stitch (see stitch diagrams) will appear on the back of the work.

4 To finish the quilt, make a 2 in/5 cm double bias binding using the continuous strip technique. Press the binding in half lengthwise. With right sides together, align the raw edges of the binding with the raw edges of the quilt. Using your machine presser foot as a seam guide (width from needle to foot edge), stitch the binding to the front of the quilt. Turn the binding over the raw edge and slipstitch the folded edge of binding to the back of the quilt.

> ❝ On small blocks I work decorative stitches in rows approximately 1 in/2.5 cm apart with stitches about ½ – ¾ in/1 – 2 cm apart. On a large quilt both rows and stitches can be spaced farther apart. I like to place the stitches "by eye" to give the work a more naïve and less organized effect, but do use chalk lines if you prefer to stitch on a guideline. ❞

DECORATIVE STITCHES QUILTING PATTERNS

Cross stitch (diagram 1)

1 Working from top to bottom, bring the needle out at **A**. Stitch from **B** to **C** through all layers.

2 Insert the needle at **D** and passing the needle through top layers only, bring it out again at a new point **A** to begin the next stitch.

Buttonhole or Blanket stitch (diagram 2)

1 Working from top to bottom, bring the needle out **A** and make a loop with thread. Stitch from **B** to **C** through all layers.

2 Insert the needle at **D** to hold the loop, then push the needle between the layers bringing the needle out at a new point **A** to begin the next stitch.

Methodist knot (diagram 3)

1 Working from right to left (similar to a backstitch), bring the needle out at **A**. Stitch from **B** to **C** through all layers.

2 Insert the needle at **D** to make a small backstitch, then push the needle between the layers, bringing it out at a new point **A** to begin the next stitch.

Mennonite tacks (diagram 4)

1 Working from right to left, bring the needle out at **A**. Stitch from **B** to **C** through all layers.
2 Take the needle back down at **D** to form a small vertical bar across the first stitch and passing the needle through top layers only, bring it out again at a new point **A** to begin the next stitch.

Fly stitch (diagram 5)

1 Working from top to bottom and spacing the stitches about 2 in/5.5 cm apart, bring the needle out at **A**, then loop the thread and stitch from **B** to **C** through all layers.

2 Take the needle back down at **D** to secure the loop of the first stitch. Passing the needle through top layers only, bring it out again at a new point **A** to begin the next stitch.

> ❝ Make these stitches about $^1/_4$ – $^3/_8$ in/6mm – 1 cm long. If they are much larger they'll look clumsy. ❞

Utility quilting (diagram 6)

This is quicker to work than traditional hand quilting and produces a softer look than machine quilting. It is extremely suitable for country quilts.

1 These small, even running stitches should be of a consistent length, between $^1/_8$ and $^1/_4$ in/3 and 6 mm. The thickness of both fabric and thread will affect the length of the stitch. Work either in straight rows as I have done or in a freehand zigzag from right to left.

diagram 1
Cross stitch

diagram 4
Mennonite tacks

diagram 2
Buttonhole stitch

diagram 5
Fly stitch

diagram 3
Methodist knot

diagram 6
Utility quilting

A PIECE OF SUMMER

*Sunny summery days are captured in this lively quilt made from reproductions
of 1930s print fabrics: bubblegum pink, lemon yellow, bright green, and tomato red with only the solid
white providing a calming influence. This is a version of Broken Dishes, a block pattern that was often used in
early quilts. If repeated blocks of this design are made from multipatterned fabrics and arranged edge to edge, they will
produce an overall effect of fragments of china. Here the pieced blocks are arranged alternately with large squares,
and this gives a strong diagonal slant to the design. The quilt is very simple and quick to piece. It took
about thirty hours. It will make a bright top quilt for a bed or a throw for a sofa.*

◆

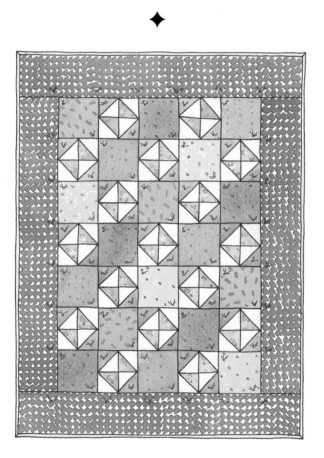

Quilt size: 52½ x 68½ in/132 x 171.5 cm

MATERIALS

All fabrics used in the quilt top are 45 in/115 cm wide.

Pieced squares: pink, 18 in/50 cm; green (**A**), 18in/
50 cm; solid white, 27 in/70 cm
Large squares: green (**B**), 9 in/25 cm; yellow, 9 in/
25 cm; blue (**A**), 9 in/25 cm; blue (**B**), 9 in/25 cm

Border: red print, 60 in/150 cm
Ribbon: woven cotton ribbon for mock ties
Batting: cotton, 72 x 56 in/184 x 145 cm
Backing: 72 x 56 in/184 x 145 cm
Binding: beige, 24 in/60 cm square

PIECED SQUARES
Cutting

1 Cut 17 pink squares, 17 green (**A**) squares, and 34 white squares, all 5 in/13 cm.

Stitching

1 Place the squares right sides together, pairing one square of either pink or green (**A**) to one white square to make 34 pairs in total.

2 Draw a pencil line diagonally from corner to corner. Machine stitch on both sides of the diagonal line (shown below), using the width from the machine needle to the edge of the presser foot as a seam allowance.

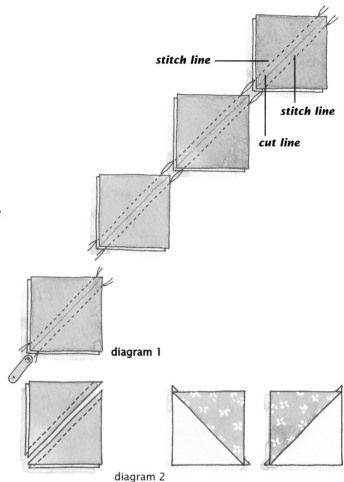

stitch line

stitch line

cut line

diagram 1

3 Repeat the process with the other squares, using the chain-piecing method. Doing this cuts out the need to break the thread and restart with each new set of squares.

4 When all the squares have been stitched, snip them apart, then cut along the diagonal lines (diagram 1). You will now have new squares made up of two triangles: one patterned and one solid white (diagram 2). Press all the seams toward the patterned fabric.

5 Trim the pieced squares to the correct size: 4½ in/11.5 cm square.

diagram 2

6 Join two pieced squares together. Press the seams toward the patterned fabric, then join the pairs (shown below).

7 Complete all 17 pieced blocks in the same way. Press the seams.

❝For step 2, place a pair of squares (white piece uppermost) on a piece of fine sandpaper to prevent the fabrics from slipping.❞

> **"**I like to make these pieced units a little on the large side, then trim them to the required size once the first machine-sewing stage has been completed.**"**

LARGE SQUARES
Cutting

1 From the remaining pieces of colored fabric, cut the large squares. These should be cut the same size as the completed pieced blocks, i.e., 8½ in/21.5 cm square. Measure the completed pieced blocks and if necessary adjust the measurement for the large squares.

2 From each of the blue fabrics (**A** and **B**), cut five large squares. From the yellow and green (**B**) fabrics, cut four large squares each.

Stitching

1 Following the quilt plan, join the blocks into rows. Press the seams away from the pieced squares. Stitch the rows together. Press the seams.

ADDING THE BORDERS

1 Determine the length of the two side borders by measuring the quilt top from center top edge to center bottom edge. From the red fabric, cut two borders to this measurement, 6½ in/16.5 cm wide.

2 Stitch the borders to the quilt sides. Press the seams toward the borders.

3 Determine the length for the top and bottom borders by measuring across the quilt top from center side edge to center side edge. From the red fabric, cut two borders to this measurement, 6½ in/16.5 cm wide.

4 Stitch the borders to the top and bottom edges of the quilt and press the seams toward the borders.

FINISHING THE QUILT

1 Cut 96 lengths of ribbon for the mock ties, each 16 in/40 cm long.

2 This ribbon will be too thick to pull through the quilt layers, so make mock ties as follows: fold the lengths in half and then in half again and tie two knots in the middle, one on top of the other. Snip through the loops at the ends.

3 Layer the quilt top, batting, and backing, and baste or pin the layers together.

4 Stitch each mock tie in place (see quilt plan) by making a firm backstitch through all quilt layers, then stitch the tie securely to the quilt; finish with a couple of backstitches hidden under the knot of the tie. Finish the quilt with a double bias binding using the continuous strip technique.

WINTER WALL

This rustic quilt was created from a variety of tweed and suiting samples arranged in a Brick Wall design. These samples originally came from the workroom of a high-class tailor and were passed on to me by a friend. The colors and textures of the tweeds evoke a strong feeling of the countryside in winter: frozen landscapes, leaden skies, and trees stripped bare of their leaves. The borders are made from a remnant of silk tweed. This warm lap quilt would give solace on a stormy night. In the past utility quilts and comforters were often made from old clothing, remnants, scraps left over from dressmaking, and fabrics saved from swatch cards. The quilts were sometimes lined with old blankets, but this one is padded with a thin batting. It took roughly twenty hours.

◆

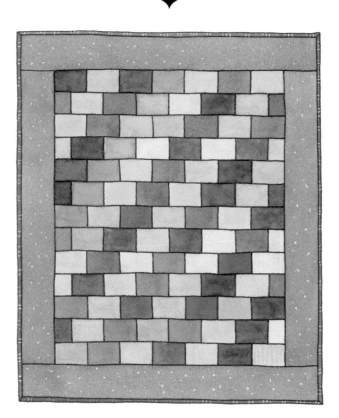

Quilt size: 54 x 61½ in/137 x 156 cm

MATERIALS

Scraps or sample fabrics: in a variety of light, medium, and dark tones, large enough to make 97 rectangles, each 6½ x 4½ in/16.5 x 11.5 cm
Small stick-on labels: for labeling the rows
Border fabric: wool, ¾ yard/70 cm, 60 in/152 cm wide
Backing: brushed cotton or similar, 64 x 58 in/163 x 148 cm (if possible, use 60 in/150 cm wide fabric for the backing as it will save joining narrower pieces)
Batting: thin, 64 x 58 in/163 x 153 cm
Quilting thread: extra strong or buttonhole thread
Needles: long needles with an eye large enough to take the thick thread

DESIGNING

Clear a space on the floor and arrange the pieces in 13 rows in a "brick wall" formation, referring to the quilt plan. You will need a total of 85 full rectangles and 12 half rectangles. Don't cut these to size yet, just tuck under the spare fabric until you are happy with the arrangement. Look again at the quilt plan on page 68 and you will see that every other row begins and ends with a half rectangle and also that I have arranged light, medium and dark rectangles in diagonal patterns.

> ❝ To view the full effect of your color arrangement, look at it through a quilters' reducing glass or through the wrong end of binoculars; this way you will quickly see if the design works. ❞

CUTTING

1 When you are happy with the arrangement, trim all the scraps to the required size. The pieces for this quilt are all 6½ x 4½ in/16.5 x 11.5 cm.

2 Cut the half rectangles to size, but don't just cut them to half the size of the full rectangles; remember that you need to allow for seam allowances. So if, for example, your large rectangle measures 6½ x 4½ in/16.5 x 11.5 cm, make the half rectangles 3½ x 4½ in/9 x 11.5 cm.

3 As you pick up the pieces for trimming, take care not disturb your design. When all the pieces have been trimmed, carefully stack the pieces in rows and use the stick-on labels to number each row. Hold the pieces for each row together with a clothespin or large clip.

STITCHING

1 Pick up one row at a time and stitch the rectangles, joining the short edges together, still keeping the pieces in strict order. Press the seams open. (Because these suiting samples are thicker than fabrics normally used for quiltmaking, it would be extremely bulky if the seams were pressed in one direction only.) Leave the label in place but do not iron on top of it as this may leave a sticky mark.

2 Replace the completed row, then pick up, stitch, and press the next one in the same way. Continue until all the rectangles have been joined, making 13 rows.

3 Stitch the rows together, again taking care not to disturb the order of the arrangement.

ADDING THE BORDERS

1 To determine the measurements for the side borders, measure across the pieced quilt top from center top to center bottom, including the seam allowances.

2 Using this measurement, cut two strips from the border fabric, each 6½ in/16.5 cm wide. Stitch one to each side of the quilt and press the seams open.

3 For the top and bottom borders, measure the quilt from center side edge to center side edge, including the seam allowances.

4 Using this measurement, cut two border strips each 6½ in/16.5 cm wide. Machine stitch to top and bottom edges of the quilt and press the seams open.

FINISHING THE QUILT

1 Center the completed quilt top carefully onto the layered backing and batting (with the batting in the middle). Make sure that you leave a clear 3 in/7.5 cm of batting and backing fabric showing on all sides beyond the edges of the quilt top. This will be used for finishing the quilt. Pin and baste through all layers.

2 Using a thick thread and large needle, quilt along the horizontal seam lines using either utility quilting or Mennonite tacks (see page 62).

3 To quilt the border, use masking tape to make guidelines and frame the pieced section of the quilt with four or five rows of utility quilting.

4 To finish the quilt, trim away excess batting and backing, leaving 2 in/5 cm showing. Fold the backing and batting over to the front of the work, aligning raw edge of backing with raw edge of quilt top. Fold over again to form a 1 in/2.5 cm final border. Baste, then finish with slipstitch or blanket stitch.

SIMPLE and SERENE

These are the two qualities in nature and the surrounding countryside that I value most and that I have incorporated into my quilts. These are also qualities much favored by the Japanese and reflected in their textile designs. This mutual interest led me to find out more about the influences on Japanese designs and motifs. The resulting ideas are reflected in these quilts.

Many Japanese live in crowded cities, due to the scarcity of habitable land on their group of islands. As genuine quiet can be hard to come by, they have developed beliefs to cultivate inner space and peace. Besides enabling them to enjoy the beauties of nature as if in private while in the midst of a crowd, this also allows them to imagine forested mountainsides when contemplating a moss-covered rock set in a serene garden only a few feet square. The majority of their motifs are inspired by natural forms. The Japanese are also very conscious of the weather and the passing seasons and will turn up en masse at specific sites to view cherry blossoms or irises in bloom.

Simple designs; inner serenity: pleasures I hope you will find while working the following quilts.

— JENNI DOBSON

PACIFIC KIMONO

Having read that Japanese nobility slept on the floor under ordinary clothing at a time roughly corresponding to the Western medieval period, I felt compelled to make a quilt that looked like a kimono for our own bed! Making a large version of Sawako Tsurugiji's charming kimono block seemed a perfect and speedy answer. This is the result; with its lightweight filling it's ideal for a bed covering in warm weather.

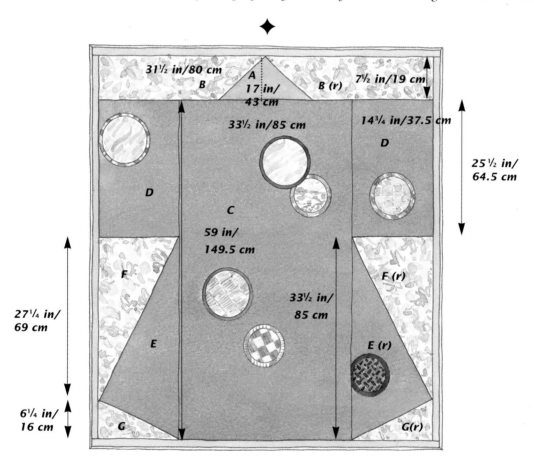

Quilt size: 68 x 71½ in/174 x 182.5 cm

MATERIALS

Dark blue fabric for kimono: (with a woven geometric design to save marking a quilting design) 4 yards/3.8 meters, 45 in/115 cm wide

Background fabric: printed cotton, 1½ yards/ 1.4 meters, 45 in/115 cm wide

Faded crimson for collar: 1 fat quarter

Border fabric: light blue, ⅝ yard/60 cm, 45 in/115 cm wide

Binding fabric: light yellow, ¼ yard/25 cm, 45 in/ 115 cm wide

Scraps of print and solid fabrics for rings, fillings and checkerboards: 11 squares for the rings and filling fabrics, none greater than 11 x 11 in/28 x 28 cm; six strips for checkerboards, none greater than 21 x 2½ in/54 x 6.5 cm.

Cardboard or template plastic

Backing: 2¼ yards/2 meters, 80 in/203 cm wide

Lightweight batting: 1 double-bed-size piece

Masking tape: 2 in/5.5 cm wide

ALTERNATIVE COLOR SCHEMES

Changing the three basic colors of the kimono block alters the balance and appearance of the design in interesting ways. Red is a felicitous color in Japan, often featured on traditional wedding kimonos (top left). Set it against a neutral gray background, with sparkling black and white fabrics for the appliqué blocks. Alternatively, choose a multicolored plaid for the kimono, with one of the darker colors for the background (top right), then find solids in the rest of the colors for the accent rings. A neutral background combined with a low-key chestnut print would make a very liveable-with quilt. Tans, rusts, and an accent of yellow lifts this color scheme out of the commonplace (left). Fresh with the coolness of the ocean, the turquoise color scheme benefits from the accent of geranium (right).

The kimono is decorated with a few simply appliquéd rings, containing strip-pieced checkerboards or just showcasing attractive pieces of fabric. Of course, the idea of working a whole quilt as a large version of one block isn't totally new – think of the Amish favorite, Diamond in a Square – but I think it's one that suits the quilter in a hurry, as the top for this quilt was assembled and decorated in two days. I made the body of the kimono using a subtle satin-woven check fabric, which eliminated the need to mark the "juji-tsunagi" sashiko design quilted across the top part of the kimono. I chose to hand quilt (not in a weekend!), but this design eminently suits machine quilting. I chose to stitch a related curved pattern, known as "chidori-tsunagi," in the lower half, but a quicker alternative would be to follow the woven lines of the fabric to machine quilt the first pattern over the whole of the kimono.

For the curious, the quilt owes its name to a visit I made to the Pacific coast of California around the towns of Carmel and Monterey. The deep blue fabric for the kimono, originally chosen for its suitability as a quilting grid, reminded me of the ocean there, and I decided to build the color scheme of the whole quilt around my memories of a beautiful day – sun-bleached rocks, faded paint on wooden buildings, etc. The seven rings scattered over this quilt are my choice – work your own to suit the fabrics you have chosen. As I quilted it, I realized that the pine trees at the top of the beach in Carmel were missing. Though it was too late to add their dark green to the color palette, because pines are such a favorite motif in Japan, I was able to quilt little stylized branches of them between the shoulders on the back of my kimono as the important back protector!

CUTTING

1 Following the measurements on the quilt plan, draw up the rectangular areas **A** - **B** and **E** - **F** - **G** on large pieces of paper and cut them apart to make patterns for shapes **A** to **F**.

2 From the dark blue kimono fabric, cut one **C** rectangle (kimono back), 34 x 59½ in/87 x 152 cm, and two **D** rectangles (sleeves), 26 x 15¼ in/67 x 39 cm.

3 Using pattern piece **E** and adding ¼ in/0.75 cm seam allowance on all sides, cut one triangle **E** and one of **E** reversed (kimono fronts), also from the dark blue.

4 From the background fabric and using the prepared patterns with ¼ in/0.75 cm seam allowance added to all sides of all pieces, cut one each of pieces **B**, **F**, and **G** and one of each in reverse: **B(r)**, **F(r)**, and **G(r)**.

5 Fold the faded crimson in half and place pattern piece **A** with the center line on the fold, then add ¼ in/0.75 cm seam allowance on outer edges and cut one collar **A**.

6 From the full width of the light blue border fabric, cut strips 2½ in/7 cm wide to be used at a later stage to make up four borders, 70 in/178 cm long.

7 For the binding, from the full width of the yellow fabric, cut strips 1 in/2.5 cm wide to a total 8 yards/7.5 meters.

8 For two 10 in/25.5 cm rings, cut four squares 11 x 11 in/ 28 x 28 cm, two of ring fabric and two of filling fabric.

9 For two 9 in/ 23 cm checkerboard rings, cut two squares 10 x 10 in/25.5 x 25.5 cm of ring fabric and two pairs of strips, each strip 21 x 2½ in/54.5 x 6.5 cm.

10 For two 8 in/20 cm rings, cut four squares 9 x 9 in/23 x 23 cm, two of ring fabric and two of filling fabric.

11 For one 7 in/18 cm checkerboard ring, cut one square 8 x 8 in/20 x 20 cm and two strips each 13 x 1½ in/35 x 4 cm.

STITCHING
Plain filled rings

1 Either using the ring patterns provided on page 77 or drawing your own with a pair of compasses, make templates from cardboard or plastic for the sizes of ring required. I have used four sizes of ring with a diameter of 7, 8, 9, and 10 in/ 18, 20, 23, and 25.5 cm. Include the vertical and horizontal register marks.

2 Iron the squares of ring and filling fabric, then finger press vertical and horizontal folds in both (shown below).

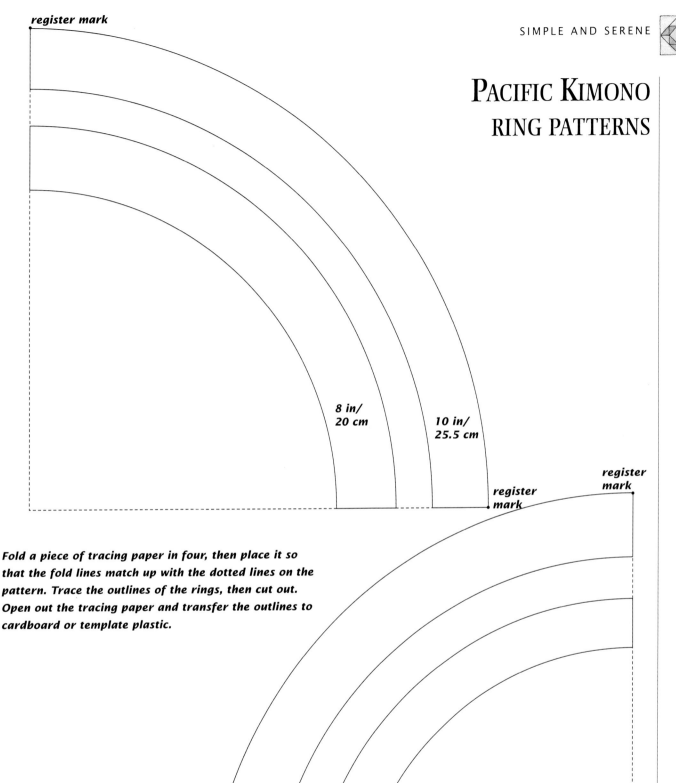

PACIFIC KIMONO
RING PATTERNS

register mark

8 in/
20 cm

10 in/
25.5 cm

register
mark

register
mark

Fold a piece of tracing paper in four, then place it so that the fold lines match up with the dotted lines on the pattern. Trace the outlines of the rings, then cut out. Open out the tracing paper and transfer the outlines to cardboard or template plastic.

9 in/
23 cm

7 in/
18 cm

register
mark

3 Line up the register marks on the ring template with these folds on the right side of the ring fabric; draw in the concentric circles of the ring (shown below).

4 Place the marked ring fabric, right side up, over the right side of the filling fabric. Pin, then baste carefully between the two concentric circles (shown below).

5 Cut away the fabric from inside the ring, leaving a scant ¼ in/0.75 cm for turning (shown below). Clip the turning allowance just near the vertical and horizontal register marks where the grain is straightest (shown top, right). If you clip all round the curve, it may stretch too much and be more difficult to stitch down neatly. Fold under the turning and blind hem.

6 After stitching the inside of the ring, use the basting stitches as a guide to trim away the excess filling fabric from just outside the basting stitches. It may help to fold lightly along the outer drawn line as a guide also.

7 Place the ring on the kimono panel of the quilt, pin and baste in place. Trim the excess fabric from around the outer ring and blind hem to the panel. Instead of stitching on the rings as you prepare them, you might like to prepare several up to step 6, then spread out the kimono panels and play with the placement of the rings to find an arrangement that pleases you. Japanese design favors having some partly hidden, either by overlapping them (as in the back panel of the kimono featured) or, rather than centering them, having some slipping into a seam (as with the ring on the right front.)

Checkerboard filled rings

The wider strips make a checkerboard to fit the 9 in/23 cm rings and the narrower strips make a checkerboard to fit the 7 in/ 18 cm ring.

1 Place a pair of strips, right sides together, and stitch with a ¼ in/0.75cm seam. Press seam toward the darker fabric.

2 Cross-cut the assembled strip into pieces of the same width as the original strips (diagram 1).

diagram 1

diagram 2

3 Stitch the pieces together in pairs, reversing the colors (diagram 2). Stitch two pairs together to make two rectangles of four-by-two squares. Press, then join these units to make a four-by-four checkerboard (shown below).

4 Use the center seam lines for registering the ring fabric over the checkerboard, then baste, trim, and blind hem the ring as before.

ASSEMBLING THE QUILT TOP
1 After stitching the rings to the panels, use the quilt plan to lay out all the pieces for the enlarged block.

2 With ¼ in/0.75 cm seam allowances, stitch the panels together as follows:
B to **A** to **Br** for unit **1**; **F** to **E**, then **G** to **E** for unit **2**; **Fr** to **Er**, then to **Gr** for unit **2r**. Press the seams.

3 Stitch one panel **D** (sleeve) to the top of unit **2** and another to unit **2r**. Press.

4 Stitch one of these to each long side of panel **C** (kimono back). Press before adding unit **1** across the top.

ADDING THE BORDERS
1 If necessary join strips to make the borders, then attach them to the completed block.

FINISHING THE QUILT
I divided the kimono featured into upper and lower parts using a zigzag line marked with ¼ in/0.75 cm masking tape. Above this I stitched the step-and-cross pattern "juji-tsunagi" following the woven grid of the fabric (shown below). The lower half I stitched with another grid design, called "chidori-tsunagi," but as a quicker alternative, I recommend that you quilt the "juji-tsunagi" design all over the kimono.

1 Assemble the three layers of backing, batting, and top, then baste or pin.

2 Machine quilt the chosen designs on the kimono. Quilt the rings in the ditch and the background with parallel lines marked using 2 in/5.5 cm wide masking tape.

3 After quilting, insert a line of permanent basting in a matching thread to hold the edges of the quilt together before attaching the binding. Sign or label to finish.

SASHIKO INSPIRATIONS 1

Inspired by sashiko stitching, originally used on working jackets for people like firefighters, fishermen, and country farmers, this crib quilt in traditional navy and white pays tribute to the technique with a mixture of hand and machine work in a quilt-as-you-stitch method. The quilt took roughly five hours apart from the quilting. I stitched mine by hand with sashiko-style stitching, but it would obviously be quicker by machine. Unlike traditional Western quilting, where the aim is to have the stitch and space next to it equal in size, in sashiko the space is as small as is practical on the fabric being used and the stitch about twice as big. This makes the technique ideal for a speedy project, and it is even quicker here because the main focus of this crib quilt is a boldy enlarged sashiko pattern interpreted in machine-couched cotton knitting yarn.

✦

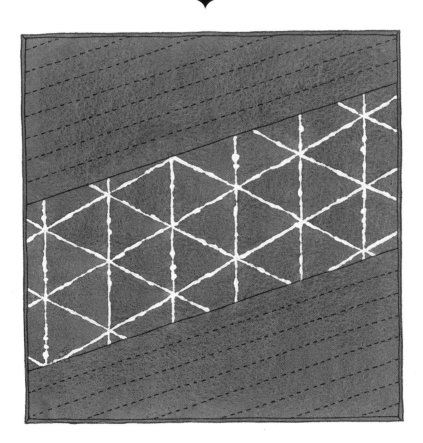

Quilt size: 34 x 34 in/86 x 86 cm

MATERIALS

All fabrics used in the quilt are 45 in/115 cm wide.
Solid navy cotton fabric: 1 yard/1 meter
Coordinating backing: 1 yard/1 meter
Batting: 1¼ yards/115 cm

Clear nylon machine-quilting thread
White, textured cotton knitting yarn: 1 skein
White sashiko thread or pearl cotton
Masking tape: 2 in/5.5 cm wide

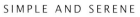
CUTTING

1 Wash and iron the navy fabric and the backing. Trim the selvages from the navy fabric, then cut five 1 in/2.5 cm wide strips from the length of the navy, parallel to the selvage. Put aside for the binding.

2 On the remaining almost-square piece of navy, mark two points: one 15 in/38 cm down from the top edge on the left-hand side and the other 6 in/15 cm down from the top edge on the right-hand side. With a yard (meter) stick and a fabric marker, connect the two points. Rule a second line parallel to the first about 14 in/35.5 cm away. Cutting along these drawn lines, divide the fabric into unequal thirds and label top, middle, and lower (shown below).

diagram 1

diagram 2

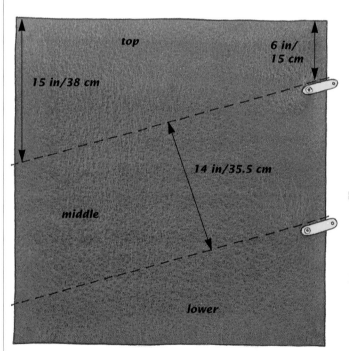

> **" "** A sharpened sliver of dried soap is good for marking the cutting lines. **" "**

MARKING THE QUILT TOP

1 Again with the stick and marker, rule the sashiko grid on the right side of the middle third. Rule the first left-hand vertical about 1¼ in/3.25 cm from the left-hand edge. Rule 6 in/15 cm lines parallel to the selvage (diagram 1).

2 On the second vertical line, mark three points each 6 in/15 cm apart. Using a quilter's rule or set square to keep marks even, repeat on every second vertical in a horizontal line with the first set.

3 With a yard (meter) stick, draw diagonal lines connecting the marks in both directions (diagram 2). Add further parallel lines to cover the whole area.

ASSEMBLING THE QUILT

1 Spread out the backing fabric, right side down, on a flat surface with the batting on top and center the marked middle third of the navy, right side up, on top. Check that the top and bottom sections will fit within the area of the backing before safety-pinning the three layers together.

MACHINE COUCHING

1 Load the sewing machine with a matching thread for the backing in the bobbin and the clear nylon thread on the top. Select the blind-hem stitch on the machine, if available. If not, select a moderately open zigzag but be aware that this will flatten the texture of the yarn more noticeably. Set the width of swing on the zigzag stitch so that it pierces the yarn rather than merely bridging it, which would allow the yarn to be pulled out (diagram 1).

diagram 1

diagram 2

2 Taking care not to stretch the cotton knitting yarn, place the end about 1 in/2.5 cm beyond the first vertical drawn line and place pins at right angles across the yarn to hold it in place down the line (diagram 2). Leave about 1 in/2.5 cm extra at the finish, then cut off. Repeat on all the vertical lines.

3 Couch the yarn in place, stitching all the lines in the same direction. Setting the stitch length to 0 for a few stitches at the start and end of each line of stitching allows you to trim the thread ends without laboriously tying them off or stitching them into the layers.

4 Repeat the process of pinning the yarn in place, then stitching it, first on one diagonal across the panel, then on the other. Remove the safety pins.

5 With right sides together, place the top third navy piece over the top edge of the middle panel so that when stitched with a ¼ in/0.75 cm seam allowance the vertical edges will be even. Pin, then stitch. Flip the top section into place over the seam and either finger press or very lightly press the seam with just the point of the iron, being careful not the crush the batting. Reposition the safety pins to hold all three layers together in the top third. Repeat with the lower third.

6 Using the sashiko thread or pearl cotton, quilt the top and lower thirds with lines of sashiko-style stitching, parallel to the diagonal seams. In the quilt shown, these lines were about 2 in/5.5 cm apart, marked with wide masking tape. If you prefer a quicker alternative, substitute machine-couched knitting yarn, as in the center section.

7 After quilting, use navy thread to put in a line of permanent basting stitches close to the edge (i.e., within the ¼ in/0.75 cm seam allowance) all around the quilt. Trim away excess backing and batting.

8 Join the binding strips, use to bind the quilt, then label to finish.

> ❝It's a good idea to work a small sample of machine couching, prepared as directed, to test the best stitch length, width, and tension for the chosen fabrics and cotton knitting yarn. The couching stitches should be unnoticeable, and the straight stitches right beside the yarn being couched.❞

SPRING WALL HANGING

The Japanese are intensely aware of nature. Certain plants are associated with different months or seasons and symbolize particular characteristics or virtues. Here we have three spring flowers: the violet, the cherry, and the iris. The diamond-shaped blocks upon which they are arranged are another popular form, also varied as a stylized cloud. The blocks took me roughly six hours to complete, then four hours for the quilting. The cutting and preparation technique took another afternoon.

◆

Quilt size: 43 x 55 in/109 x 139.5 cm

MATERIALS

Light gray fabric: 1¼ yards/1.2 meters, 45 in/115 cm wide

Inner border fabric: two solid greens, ⅛ yard/10 cm each, 45 in/115 cm wide

Outer border fabric: cotton printed home furnishings fabric, ¾ yard/70 cm, 48 in/120 cm wide

Thin paper for tracing the blocks or photocopies

Paper-backed fusible webbing: 1½ yards/1.4 meters

Flowers, centers, and leaves: mixed print and solid scraps

Block background fabrics: seven scrap pieces, none larger than 10 x 7 in/26 x 18 cm

Baking parchment paper

Lightweight interfacing: 1 yard/1 meter

Binding fabric: bright yellow, ¼ yard/30 cm, 45 in/ 115 cm wide

Batting: 1¾ yards/1.75 meters, 60 in/150 cm wide

Backing: 1¾ yards/1.75 meters, 60 in/150 cm wide

Masking tape: ⅝ in/1.75 cm and ¼ in/0.75 cm

Machine-embroidery threads

The blocks have been worked using fusible webbing and mounted onto a support of lightweight interfacing. They are most efficiently worked as a set, all the cutting and bonding being done first, before working the satin stitch. Only scraps of fabric are needed for the motifs. Limiting the number of threads for the embroidery will unify a diversity of scraps. The blocks are scattered over a simple, framed background, which is machine quilted in parallel lines, the narrow ones with added bar tacks to represent bamboo, another Japanese favorite plant, symbolizing endurance and constancy.

CUTTING

1 From the light gray fabric, cut a rectangle 31 x 42¾ in/ 79 x 108.5 cm.

2 Cut two strips from across the width of both solid green fabrics for the inner border, each 1 in/2.5 cm wide.

3 From across the width of the printed outer border fabric, cut four strips 6 in/15 cm wide.

4 Enlarge the block designs provided on pages 88 and 89 to measure 9 in/23 cm across the widest point on each diamond. Turn each design over, label this the working side, and ink over all design lines to give the reverse pattern required. Note that the second cherry design is used twice, once in reverse.

5 Place the fusible webbing, paper side up, over the working side of one design and trace all parts of the design separately, including the background diamond shape (shown below). Leaves and petals butt up together, but the background shape should be a complete outline so that it goes behind the flowers and leaves.

6 Carefully cut out each of the separate leaves and flowers from the fusible webbing tracings, then cut out a separate piece for the diamond background shape. Place each shape web side down in turn on the wrong side of the chosen fabric and bond.

7 Cut out the bonded shapes (shown below) and save all the pieces for the block in an envelope. Repeat to prepare all seven of the appliqué blocks.

8 From the interfacing, cut one rectangle 11 x 6½ in/ 28 x 17 cm for the iris block, and six rectangles, each 10 x 7 in/25 x 18 cm, for the other blocks.

9 From across the width of the bright yellow binding fabric, cut five strips, 1½ in/4 cm wide, and join.

STITCHING

1 Working a block at a time, remove the backing paper from the fused diamond background fabric and bond it to a rectangle of interfacing, following the manufacturer's instructions. Allow to cool before handling. Remove the backing papers from the rest of the shapes for this block, position them correctly, using the original paper pattern as a guide, then bond. Work all blocks to this stage (shown below).

2 Set the sewing machine to work a satin stitch, making a sample first to check the tension. Work all the satin stitches around the outlines of all flowers, leaves, and diamonds. Try to plan so that each new color will cover the ends of the preceding one. Where possible, work all of one color where it appears on different blocks. It isn't necessary to have exactly matching threads for each fabric, as repeating a color helps unify the designs. Cut out each completed block from the interfacing.

ADDING THE BORDERS

1 Stitch the two lighter green inner border strips to the left-hand side and the top of the light gray rectangle.

2 Stitch the two darker green strips to the right-hand side and the bottom.

3 Attach the outer border strips to the sides of the quilt, trimming the ends even as necessary. Add the outer borders to the top and bottom.

FINISHING THE QUILT

1 Turn over a prepared diamond block, place fusible webbing, paper side up, on top and trace the block outline, being sure to go right to the edges of the block behind the outer stitching (shown below). Cut out and fuse to the back of the block. Repeat for all blocks.

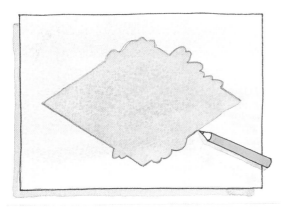

2 Preferably hang the prepared quilt background and pin the blocks in a pleasing arrangement over it. You don't have to copy my design, but note the asymmetry and use of a diagonal flow, both features of Japanese design. Also consider the space around and between the blocks, as this is more important to the Japanese eye than the blocks themselves. When you have an arrangement you like, take the quilt down, peel off the backing paper and bond each block in position to the background. Allow each to cool before moving the background to attach the next.

3 Assemble the quilt top, batting, and backing ready for quilting.

4 Using $5/8$ in/1.75 cm wide masking tape, mark the bold quilting lines at interesting angles and intervals. Avoid getting them all leaning at the same degree or too equally spaced – the effect you are representing is a stand of bamboo stalks. Also leave space for the narrower stalks.

5 Using a walking or even-feed foot if available and machine-embroidery thread, quilt along both edges of the masking tape, taking care not to stitch through it and always working from the top of the quilt down. Don't be tempted to turn the quilt and work some from the other direction as this may cause ripples.

6 Remove the masking tape promptly and mark some narrower stalks with $1/4$ in/0.75 cm wide masking tape. Quilt along both edges of these, then remove the tape. At intervals on the narrow stalks stitch a bar tack, but without tightening the thread, to represent the joints in the bamboo.

7 Trim the backing and batting even with the outer border of the quilt top and check that the corners are true. Stitch the bright yellow binding strips to the quilt $3/8$ in/1 cm from the edge. Fold over to the back of the work, turning in the raw edge, and blind hem to a finished $3/8$ in/1 cm.

8 Make and attach a hanging sleeve, then sign or label your quilt to finish.

SPRING WALL HANGING
BLOCK DESIGNS

.... *dotted lines indicate the complete background outline*

- - - - *dashed lines indicate surface stitching*

violet 1

violet 2

violet 3

cherry 1

cherry 2

iris

SASHIKO INSPIRATIONS 2

This crib quilt, inspired by a sashiko pattern very similar to that used for Sashiko Inspirations I, acknowledges other Japanese influences. First, the homespun-looking plaid reflects Japanese textile traditions. Its geometric design also eases the task of marking the quilting pattern. Second, the light batting used in the main part of the quilt (the current preference for baby covers is that they shouldn't be too warm) is balanced by a wide, padded border imitating the padded hems seen on some ceremonial kimonos. The sashiko grid, "kagome," is quickly stitched using the longest possible stitch on the machine. Worked in a matching thread, it's so low key that the stars – formed by whip stitching some of the grid lines with contrasting embroidery thread – appear as if by magic! The quilt took me approximately seven hours to complete.

◆

Quilt size: 36 x 42 in/91.5 x 106.5 cm

MATERIALS

All fabrics used in the quilt are 45 in/115 cm wide.

Plaid fabric: cotton, 1 yard/1 meter (This could be a stripe if plaids are difficult to find.)
Batting: lightweight, 1¾ yards/1.6 meters

Backing: 1 yard/1 meter
Solid putty fabric: 1 yard/1 meter
Masking tape
Embroidery thread: to contrast with plaid

CUTTING

1 From the plaid fabric, cut a rectangle 30½ x 36 in/
77.5 x 91.5 cm and matching pieces of batting and backing.

2 From solid putty fabric, cut two border strips 7½ x 44 in/
19 x 112 cm and two strips 7½ x 38 in/19 x 96.5 cm. Cut
matching pieces of batting.

STITCHING

1 Press the backing, then place, right side down, on a flat
surface. Center over it the batting and the ironed plaid, right side
up. Pin, then baste the layers together.

2 On one long side of the plaid, mark the center using a line in
the pattern as a guide. Identify other lines of the pattern at
roughly 4 in/10 cm intervals, working away from the center in
both directions (shown below, left). Set your machine for the
longest possible stitch, then machine quilt down each of these
lines in matching thread.

3 Now find the middle of the quilt on one short side. Mark this
point with pins inserted across the quilt on alternate lines of
quilting. At roughly 4 in/10 cm intervals, up and down on the
same grid lines, mark more intersections. Place strips of masking
tape to connect the pin-marked points diagonally, then machine
quilt these lines (shown top, right). Remove the tape and
reposition to connect the same points on the other diagonal.
Machine quilt.

4 Quilt a final set of lines, parallel to the very first set (shown
below, left) and halfway between them (shown below, right).

ADDING THE BORDERS

1 Mark a line parallel to and 3 in/7.5 cm in from one long edge
on each border strip. Place the batting strips on the wrong side of
the border strips and pin or baste. With the machine still set on a
long stitch, machine baste the marked lines in matching thread.
This stitching is to prevent the batting from moving during use
and will remain in the border. Machine baste again on normal
stitch length close to both edges.

2 Find the midpoint of each side of the quilt and its respective border. Pin two opposite borders to opposite sides of the center with right sides facing, taking a ¹⁄₄ in/0.75 cm seam allowance and starting and stopping stitching ¹⁄₄ in/0.75 cm from the corners (shown below). Make sure that the machine-basting line across the border will be folded over to the back of the quilt. Folding these borders out of the way where possible, attach the remaining two borders in the same manner. Again start and stop stitching ¹⁄₄ in/0.75 cm from the corners.

2 Fold the borders over to the back of the quilt, turning in ¹⁄₄ in/0.75 cm to enclose the raw edges. Fold and stitch miters at the corners on the back as you go.

3 With contrast colored embroidery thread, whip some of the grid lines to pick out some star shapes (shown below). Push the eye of the needle through first to avoid catching any fabric. To keep to Japanese design ideals, work an odd number of stars in an asymmetrical arrangement.

FINISHING THE QUILT

1 Fold the excess fabric at the corners of the borders into miters and stitch. Check that each miter lies neatly before trimming the excess batting and fabric.

GATEWAYS TO THE PAST

The overall design of this wall hanging is inspired by the Japanese "screen of state": long hanging panels used to create an illusion of privacy by dividing large rooms yet still allowing people to come and go easily. You can adapt the width or length to suit a given space by adding more panels as well as varying their width. Though this example was made from a gift collection of vintage kimono fabrics, they aren't essential to make this hanging. However, the ancient religion of Shinto holds that everything has a spirit; consequently, the Japanese feel that reusing old fabrics means their spirit is being preserved. In the past people made gifts of good fragments from worn kimonos to shrines, sometimes to be made into patched robes for monks and sometimes into altar hangings. This prompted the use of a stylized "torii," or shrine gateway, as a feature block.

◆

Quilt size: 47½ x 36 in/120.5 x 91.5 cm

MATERIALS

Torii shapes, backgrounds, and strips: about 1¾ yards/1.7 meters assorted scraps for piecing, of which five pieces must be about 11 x 9 in/28 x 23 cm

Backing: cotton printed home furnishings fabric 1⅛ yards/1 meter, 48 in/122 cm wide

Thin paper for tracing the block foundations or photocopies

Batting: needle-punched or compressed, 1⅛ yards/ 1 meter, 60 in/150 cm wide

Binding and hanging sleeves: deep red fabric, 1 yard/ 1 meter, 45 in/115 cm wide

Bamboo pole for hanging: to combined length of panels plus 6 in/15 cm

I took roughly ten hours to do the preparing, block construction, and finishing of the panels and a day to do the strip piecing. Your timing will depend on how long it takes you to assemble and organize the strips.

I decided to theme the panels around different seasons, weather, and times of the day. The first panel represents winter and snow. The second shows spring – the dawning of a new year – and the dawn of a new day. The center panel represents the height of summer and of the day. Panel four is for autumn, with its foggy evenings. The last panel shows us winter and dark, rainy nights. When assembling your own fabrics, try to choose colors and designs associated with the appropriate season but remember not to agonize over every strip. It is only symbolic.

The backing for these panels is cut from a single piece of home furnishings fabric, making them reversible should you wish to use them as a divider. The "torii" are stitched to paper foundations, which are both easy and quick to work. The rest of each panel is filled with simple strip piecing, a great way to display lots of scraps of wonderful fabrics.

> 66 If you have never used the foundation piecing method before, make a practice block first from scrap fabrics. Use a short stitch length on the machine, about 15 stitches per inch or 1.75 mm long, so the paper is easy to remove. 99

CUTTING

1 Divide the home furnishings fabric into five panels, each 9½ in/24 cm wide, and number them so that you can keep them in the right order. If your fabric is slightly less than this width, divide it equally and so make the hanging slightly narrower. Reduce the width of the "torii" block to the same measurement (most easily done on a photocopier). Mark out the 36 in/91.5 cm length on the panels but do not cut to size yet as the horizontal piecing may cause a slight alteration of the length. Cut pieces of batting to match.

2 From the deep red fabric, cut 12 strips 1 in/2.5 cm wide across the full width of the cloth. Put aside for the binding. From this fabric also cut five hanging sleeves, each 9½ x 8 in/ 24 x 20 cm. The remaining fabrics will be cut as they are needed during the making of the panels.

STITCHING
Preparation

1 Lay the panels of home furnishings fabric right side down and place a piece of batting on each. Pin, then baste lengthwise in three rows, without knots, so that the thread is easy to remove.

2 Make five tracings or photocopies of the "torii" block on page 97. Divide into four parts as shown below. These do not have seam allowances. Note that the blocks are stitched following the drawn lines but the fabrics are placed on the unmarked side of the paper. Add the numbers to the master block.

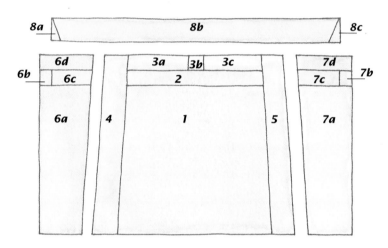

Working the foundation-pieced blocks

1 Choose two fabrics, one for the "torii" and one for the background, which you may like to think of as sky. Begin with the central part of the block. Place a piece of background (sky) fabric over the large area **1** on the plain (unmarked) side of the paper. Hold up to the light if desired, to check that the fabric covers the whole of area **1** with at least ¼ in/0.75 cm extra all around for seam allowances. Pin, then baste (shown below).

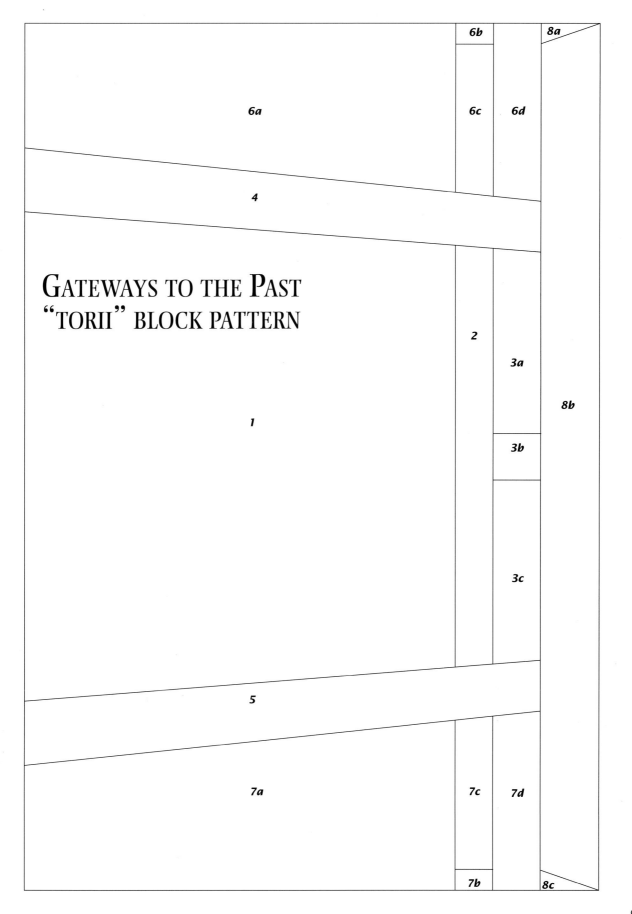

6b

8a

6a

6c

6d

4

GATEWAYS TO THE PAST
"TORII" BLOCK PATTERN

2

3a

8b

1

3b

3c

5

7a

7c

7d

8c

7b

2 Place a strip of "torii" fabric (to become piece **2**) along the top edge of the background fabric, right sides together, also with sufficient seam allowances, and pin (diagram 1). Turn the paper over and stitch along the drawn seam, starting ¼ in/0.75 cm before the drawn line and continuing the same amount beyond it (diagram 2). Turn back to the fabric side and flip the "torii" fabric right side up. Lightly press with a dry iron. Trim excess from seam allowance below to leave ¼ in/0.75 cm seam allowance.

diagram 1

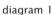

diagram 2

3 Join a 1 in/2.5 cm wide strip of "torii" (**3b**) fabric between two strips of background (**3a and 3c**) and press. Place this right side down with the insert centered on the previous "torii" strip (**2**), pin (shown top, right), then turn to the stitching side and stitch. As before, turn back to flip the latest strip right side up and press. Again trim excess from turnings below.

4 Add a strip of "torii" fabric (**4** and **5**) to each side of the center as shown below right. Notice that these strips are set slightly on the diagonal, and when placing them be sure the strips are wide enough to cover the top and bottom of the pattern plus enough for seam allowances. After pressing, trim all three sides to include ¼ in/0.75 cm seam allowance ready for stitching to the next units.

5 In a similar way, work the two side units. Place **6a** first, just as piece **1** on the center section. Piece a scrap of background (**6b**) to a strip of "torii" fabric (**6c**) before attaching to the top edge, then add strip **6d** to the top. Be sure to stitch on the lines (**6 a-d**). Repeat to make the second side unit (**7 a-d**) as shown on page 99, top. Trim to include ¼ in/0.75 cm seam allowances on all sides.

6 Work the top unit by placing "torii" fabric (**8b**) over the whole strip and piecing tiny triangles of background on both ends (**8a, c**) as shown below. Trim to include ¼ in/0.75 cm seam allowances on all sides.

7 Join the side units to the center, taking ¼ in/0.75 cm seams, and press. Add the top unit and press. Tear away the paper foundations. Repeat to work a total of five blocks.

FINISHING THE HANGING

1 If possible pin the panels, in the correct order for the printed design on the backing but with batting side facing you, on a design wall. If you don't have one of these, each panel can be pegged or pinned to a wire coat hanger and hung from picture wire. Decide where the blocks will be on each one. Remember that although you want a balanced arrangement, this does not have to be symmetrical. Pin temporarily in place.

2 Make sure the block is straight before basting in position on the panel along the short sides within the turnings.

3 Work strip piecing above and below the basted blocks to fill the rest of each panel. To speed the work, I suggest choosing a group of fabrics for each panel and cutting a few strips of varying widths from each of them. Include some tapered strips, as their angles add more interest to the finished piece. Angled strips need to be slightly longer so that when flipped right side up they cover the width of the panel completely.

4 Place the first strip, right side down, at either the top or the bottom edge of the block on the strip. Machine stitch through all layers (shown below). Flip the strip right side up and lightly press. Place a few pins at right angles along the sides before putting the next strip right side down on top and repeating the process. Continue until all the panels are filled.

5 Measure the length of the panels and re-mark the 36 in/ 91.5 cm length if necessary. Baste along the short ends of the panels within the seam allowance. Trim away excess batting and backing from all panels.

6 Join the binding strips and use to bind the panels. Turn over and blind hem to finish ¼ in/0.75 cm wide.

7 Add a hanging sleeve to the back of each panel, then thread onto the hanging pole.

PIONEER BLANKETS

Quiltmaking has come full circle with the current use of homespuns, double-brushed flannels, and wools. There has been a return to simple quilts made for everyday use in place of quilts that will become treasured heirlooms.

The nature of these types of fabric does not allow for intricate piecing or for fine hand quilting, so they are ideal for the novice quilter or the quilter in a hurry. The fabric is softer, thicker, and more loosely woven than the cottons to which we have recently become accustomed. Since the fabrics are thicker, it is advisable to use a very fine batting. Flannels and wools are nevertheless fun to work with and produce wonderfully cozy quilts to snuggle up in on cold winter days. The quilts in this section take their inspiration from the blankets used and traded by the American pioneers.

—ANNE WALKER

PIONEER PATCHES

*The early pioneers found themselves making quilts that were warm, quick,
and easy, as they set off in search of new lands and a new life. Guidebooks for the times suggested
that settlers should take with them a good number of quilts to sustain them throughout their journey.
Many of the pioneers experienced hard times on their travels; their quilts were used for bedding, shelter, and often
burial wraps. These simple, hard-wearing quilts were made from leftover suiting, tailors' samples, or, in fact, anything
that was available. This quilt tries to achieve the look of an early pioneer's quilt. I used sample fabric swatches
in a range of complementary colors and assembled the quilt in about eight hours. You could use swatches or
any fabric that you may have on hand. If you need to purchase the fabric, the number of color variations
will have to be reduced in order to keep the cost realistic, but a pleasing result can still
be achieved. This size makes a cozy lap quilt or sofa throw.*

◆

Quilt size: 48 x 60 in/ 120 x 150 cm

MATERIALS

Suiting/wool blends: 11 different fabrics, ⅓ yard /
30 cm each, 45 in/115 cm wide
Backing: 3 yards/2.7 meters, 45 in/115 cm wide

Binding: ½ yard/50 cm, 45 in/115 cm wide
Batting: fine, 52 x 64 in/130 x 160 cm
Quilting thread: soft cotton embroidery thread

ALTERNATIVE COLOR SCHEMES

These four color schemes feature different types of fabric and a variety of color ranges and designs to show how dramatically you can alter the overall look. Choose a monochromatic theme and use a large selection of tones in one color scheme. This one is "red" but uses fabric from pink to burgundy (top left).

Alternatively, use the design to show off a collection of hand-dyed fabrics in all sorts of colors and designs (top right). The design lends itself to warm, cozy flannels as in the original: this interpretation uses some patterned fabrics (left). For an alternative plain and simple design, choose strong Amish colors to give a characteristically striking color scheme (right).

CUTTING

1 If you are using samples or scraps, cut 64 squares measuring 6½ in/16.5 cm and 144 squares measuring 2½ in/6.5 cm. Alternatively from each of the 11 fabrics, cut one 6½ in/16.5 cm strip and one 2½ in/6.5 cm strip and subcut both strips into squares.

2 Cut the backing fabric in half and stitch together to form a rectangle 54 x 90 in/130 x 230 cm. From this cut a rectangle 52 x 64 in/130 x 160 cm.

3 Cut the binding fabric into strips 2½ in/7 cm wide.

STITCHING

1 Lay out a set of nine small squares to form a Nine Patch: try to ensure that no two pieces of fabric are the same. Lay another 15 sets down on top to form a stack of Nine Patches; number each stack (shown below).

2 Flip square **2** onto square **1**, right sides together, and stitch with an exact ¼ in/0.75 cm seam. Continue to chain piece all the **2**s to the **1**s. Do not cut apart (shown above, right).

> **66** When working with wools, clean the lint from your sewing machine regularly. **99**

3 Chain piece all the **3**s to the **2**s (shown below, right). Cut apart and press the seams toward the center square. Lay down in position again.

4 Chain piece **4**, **5**, and **6** in the same way. Cut apart and press toward the outside squares. Lay down in position.

5 Chain piece **7**, **8**, and **9** in the same way. Cut apart and press toward the center square. Lay down in position.

6 Join the horizontal rows to complete the Nine Patch blocks. Press the seams in one direction.

7 Lay out the plain squares and the Nine Patches as shown in the quilt plan. Try to avoid having the same fabrics touching.

8 Piece each row horizontally. Press the seams on odd rows to the left and even rows to the right. Stitch the rows together, matching seams where appropriate. Press all these seams in one direction.

FINISHING THE QUILT

1 Layer the backing, batting, and quilt top. Pin and baste in a grid, starting from the center.

2 Quilt in a pattern of your choice. I have quilted by hand in a diagonal pattern through the center of the squares using soft embroidery cotton and utility quilting (see page 62). Machine quilting the same design or tying the quilt would both work well and be quicker.

3 When the quilting is completed, trim excess backing and batting, stitch the binding strips together to the length required, and use to bind the quilt with a double-fold binding.

STAR AND STRIPES

As the pioneers moved westward, they settled in lands that had hitherto been the domain of the Native American. Early trappers and mountain men made contact with the tribes, and trade that had started with the Hudson Bay Company flourished. With the demise of the buffalo, blankets took on greater importance, replacing the buffalo robes worn on ceremonial occasions by the Native American. The simplest blanket was one with bands of color at each end. The blankets were double woven and often contained reversed colors. This simple reversible top quilt reflects these ideas and can be made, except for the hand quilting (which takes about five hours), in roughly four hours.

◆

Quilt size: 45 x 60 in/115 x 152 cm

MATERIALS

All fabrics used in the quilt are 45 in/115 cm wide.

Two main solid-colored soft flannel fabrics for front and back: 1½ yards/1.5 meters each

Three contrasting solid-colored soft flannel fabrics for the bands: ⅓ yard/30 cm each
Batting: fine, 45 x 70 in/115 x 180 cm
Binding: ½ yard/50 cm, 45 in/115 cm wide
Quilting thread: soft embroidery cotton

CUTTING

1 From each of the main fabrics, cut one 45 x 40½ in/ 115 x 104 cm rectangle and two 45 x 4 in/115 x 10.5 cm strips.

2 From each of the contrasting fabrics, cut four 45 x 2½ in/ 115 x 7.5 cm strips.

3 From the batting, cut one 45 x 40½ in/115 x 104 cm rectangle; six 45 x 2½ in/115 x 7.5 cm strips and two 45 x 4 in/115 x 10.5 cm strips.

4 Cut the binding fabric into strips 2½ in/7 cm wide.

STITCHING

1 Take the large rectangles of flannel and batting and make a sandwich with the batting in the middle and the flannels right sides out. Pin and baste in a grid, working from the center out.

2 Using a zigzag stitch, stitch round the outside to close all four sides of the rectangle.

3 Take two strips of the first contrast fabric. Lay one underneath the long edge of the rectangle, right sides together and raw edges aligned, and one on top of the long edge, right sides together and raw edges aligned. On the top of this lay a single strip of 2½ in/ 7.5 cm batting. Pin together (shown below).

4 Stitch through all layers along top edge with an exact ¼ in/ 0.75cm seam allowance. Neaten the raw edge of the seam with a zigzag stitch (shown top, right).

5 Flip the fabric strips upward, sandwiching the batting between the two strips. Pin together (shown below) and neaten the raw edge with a zigzag stitch.

6 Take two of the second contrasting fabric strips and another strip of batting and apply to the edge of the first strip, flipping and stitching as before (shown below). Repeat for the third contrasting fabric strip.

7 Take one strip of each of the main fabrics and the 4 in/ 10.5 cm wide batting strip and stitch in the same manner to the third contrasting strip.

8 Following the quilt plan, repeat all these steps to complete the other end of the quilt to match.

66 The fabric sandwich for the central portion has already been tacked in a grid, so is now ready to quilt. 99

FINISHING THE QUILT

1 Quilt in the pattern of your choice. I quilted a radiant star motif with soft embroidery cotton using a utility quilting stitch (see page 62). The star is made up of eight diamonds broken down into smaller diamonds (shown below).

2 When the quilting is completed, stitch the binding strips together to make the length required and use to bind the quilt with a double-fold binding.

STAR AND STRIPES QUILTING PATTERN

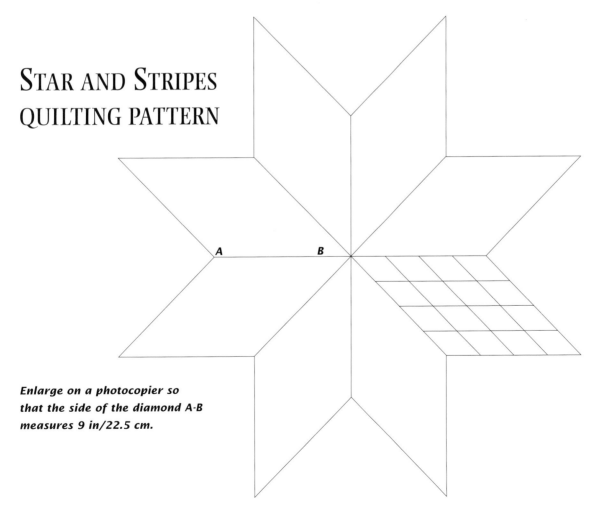

Enlarge on a photocopier so that the side of the diamond A-B measures 9 in/22.5 cm.

NAVAJO

Navajo weavers often wove designs similar in look to Florentine or bargello tapestry. Blanket manufacturers took this design idea and created similar allover woven designs in their blankets made for trading. This wool quilt, which can be made in about eighteen hours, takes the idea and creates a bargello-style lap quilt with a Navajo feel.

◆

A B C D E F G H I J K L M N O P Q R S

Quilt size: 48 x 66 in/114 x 144 cm

MATERIALS

Solid wool fabric: six different colors, ½ yard /50 cm each, 60 in/150 cm wide
Binding: ½ yard/50 cm, 60 in/150 cm wide

Backing: 52 x 70 in/124 x 154 cm. (I used 45 in/ 115 cm wide flannel. Take 4 yards/3.1meters, cut and join and cut out a rectangle of the required size.)
Batting: fine, 52 x 70 in/124 x 154 cm

CUTTING

1 From each of the six solid wool fabrics, cut three strips 6 in/13.5 cm wide.

2 Cut the binding fabric into strips 2½ in/7 cm wide.

STITCHING

1 Lay out one strip from each of the six fabrics in the order that you like best.

2 Stitch three sets of six, using an accurate ¼ in/0.75 cm seam (shown below).

3 Fold a set of stitched strips in half, right sides together and with the fold toward you, then subcut 3 in/7.5 cm strips at right angles to the seam (shown below).

4 Join two strips end to end (shown below). Continue to join strips until you have 19 strips, 12 units long.

5 Set three of these strips to one side. Join the ends of each of the remaining 16 strips until you have 16 stitched circles (shown below).

6 Undo each of the circles at a different seam to form new strips, following the chart below. So, take the first circle and unpick the seam between fabric **4** and fabric **3**. Lay out the strip with fabric **4** at the top and fabric **3** at the bottom.

	Top fabric	**Bottom fabric**
Row A	4	3
Row B	5	4
Row C	6	5
Row D	1	6 (this is one of the reserved strips)
Row E	6	5
Row F	5	4
Row G	4	3
Row H	5	4
Row I	6	5
Row J	1	6 (this is the second reserved strip)
Row K	6	5
Row L	5	4
Row M	4	3
Row N	5	4
Row O	6	5
Row P	1	6 (this is the last of the reserved strips)
Row Q	6	5
Row R	5	4
Row S	4	3

7 Continue in this way following the sequence shown in the chart, then lay out the strips in the order shown on the quilt plan, starting from the left. Press odd rows with the seams facing up and even rows with the seams facing down.

8 Join all the rows in order, starting from the left and matching all horizontal seams as you go. Press in one direction.

FINISHING THE QUILT

1 Layer the backing, batting, and quilt top. Pin and baste the layers together in a grid, starting from the center and working outward.

2 Quilt in the pattern of your choice. I have machine quilted in the ditch, but tying would also give a nice appearance.

3 When the quilting is completed, stitch the binding strips together to the length required and use to bind the quilt with a double-fold binding.

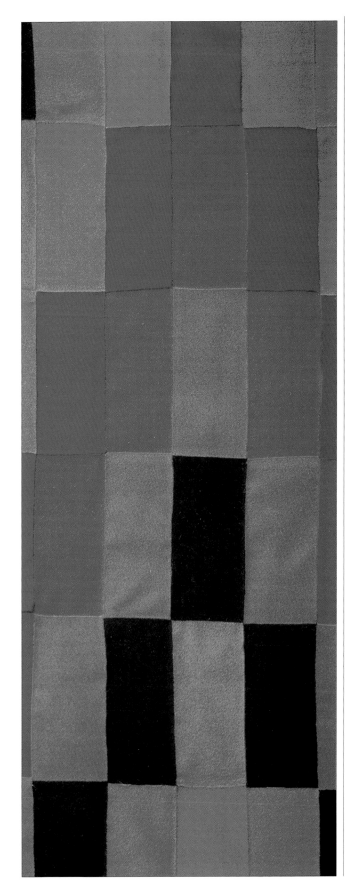

COVERED FIRE

J. Capps and Son made a name for themselves with their trading blankets featuring many-banded designs, which had patterns woven into the stripes. "Buffalo Bill" Cody described wrapping up in a Capps blanket as a realization of "a dream of the far prairie and a covered fire." This quilt uses the banded design idea and is constructed from 60 in/150 cm wide felted wool. It can be made in about twenty-four hours. This is the traditional size, as it was the maximum size that could be woven on the looms, and so makes a perfect blanket for a single bed.

◆

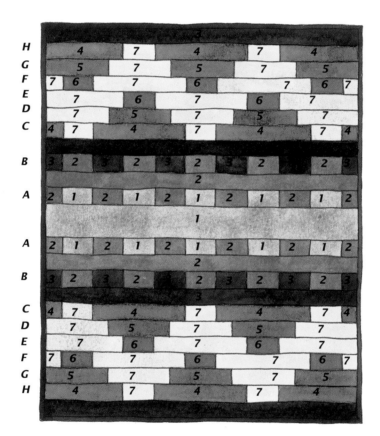

Quilt size: 60 x 72 in/150 x 180 cm

MATERIALS

Solid color fabrics 60 in/150 cm wide: Fabric 1, ½ yard/50 cm long; Fabric 2: ½ yard/50 cm long; Fabric 3: ¾ yard/70 cm long; Fabric 4: ½ yard/50 cm long; Fabric 5: ⅜ yard/35 cm long; Fabric 6: ¼ yard/25 cm long; Fabric 7: ⅞ yard/75 cm long
Binding: flannel, ½ yard/50 cm, 45 in/115 cm wide

Backing: 64 x 76 in/160 x 190 cm (I used 45 in/115 cm wide flannel. Take 4¼ yards/3.8 meters, cut and join to create the required size.)
Batting: fine, 64 x 76 in/160 x 190 cm

CUTTING

1 From fabric **1**, cut one strip 6½ in/16.5cm wide and two strips 3½ in/9 cm wide, subcut into 6½ in/16.5 cm rectangles.

2 From fabric **2**, cut two strips 3½ in/9 cm wide. Cut three more strips 3½ in/9 cm and subcut these to get 18 rectangles 6½ in/16.5 cm long and four squares measuring 3½ in/9 cm.

3 From fabric **3**, cut four strips 3½ in/9 cm wide. Cut two more strips 3½ in/9 cm wide and subcut these to get eight rectangles 6½ in/16.5 cm long and four squares measuring 3½ in/9 cm.

4 From fabric **4**, cut four strips 3½ in/9 cm wide and subcut to get four squares 3½ in/9 cm, six rectangles 18½ in/43.5 cm long, and four rectangles 15½ in/36.5 cm long.

5 From fabric **5**, cut three strips 3½ in/9 cm wide and subcut to get ten rectangles 12½ in/29.5 cm long.

6 From fabric **6**, cut two strips 3½ in/9 cm wide and subcut to get ten rectangles 6½ in/16.5 cm long.

7 From fabric **7**, cut eight strips 3½ in/9 cm wide and subcut to get ten rectangles 6½ in/16.5 cm long, ten rectangles 12½ in/29.5 cm long, six rectangles 18½ in/43.5 cm long, four rectangles 15½ in/36.5 cm long, and four squares measuring 3½ in/9 cm.

8 Cut the binding into strips 2½ in/7 cm wide.

STITCHING

1 Consulting the quilt plan at all times, lay out two lots of row **A**. Join the pieces, chain piecing where possible, using a ¼ in/0.75 cm seam allowance; press the seams open to cope with the thickness of the wool.

2 Lay out two lots of row **B**, join and press all the seams open as before. Continue in this manner until you have two rows of **C**, **D**, **E**, **F**, **G**, and **H**.

3 Lay out all the rows in the order shown in the quilt plan, including the unpieced rows, and stitch half of the quilt top from the center outward, lining up the seams as you go.

4 Complete the remainder of the quilt top to match. Press all the seams open.

FINISHING THE QUILT

1 Layer the backing, batting, and quilt top. Pin and baste in a grid, starting from the center.

2 Quilt in a pattern of your choice. I have quilted in the ditch by machine.

3 When the quilting is completed, stitch the binding strips together to the length required and use to bind the quilt with a double-fold binding.

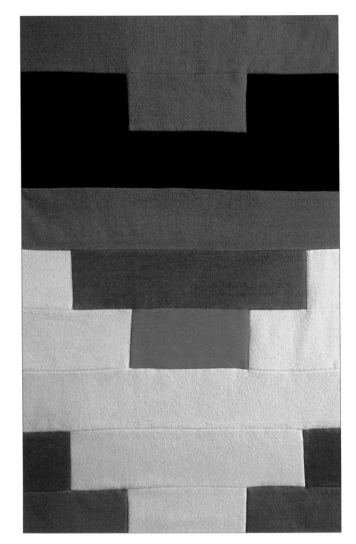

OREGON CORNHUSK
PATTERNS

Instructions for using the patterns are given on pages 118-120

small rectangle, finished size: 5 x 10 cm

large rectangle, finished size: 7.5 x 15 cm

OREGON CORNHUSK

*This single-bed quilt has more complicated piecing than the other projects in this section,
so will take roughly thirty hours to make. However, the style of the quilt completes the study of trade blankets
as a design source. Trade blanket designs were often made up of six or nine elements. These elements translate directly
for the quiltmaker into blocks. Native Americans in the plateau region, which includes Oregon, wove bags to carry
berries, fish, etc., that they had gathered or hunted. Many of these bags were embellished with geometric designs
using cornhusks, hence the name of this quilt. These designs often included a rectangle split into two long
thin triangles. These triangles can be produced quickly using the BiRangle™.*

◆

Quilt size: 54 x 60 in/135 x 150 cm

MATERIALS

All fabrics used in the quilt top are 45 in/115 cm wide.

Fabric A: solid blue, 1 yard/1 meter
Fabric B: print blue, 1 yard/1 meter
Fabric C: solid red, 1 yard/1 meter
Fabric D: solid light brown, 2 yards/2 meters

Fabric E: print green, ½ yard/50 cm
Fabric F: solid green, 1 yard/1 meter
Backing: 58 x 64 in/140 x160 cm
Batting: fine, 58 x 64 in/140 x 160 cm
Binding: ½ yard/50 cm, 45 in/115 cm wide

As the BiRangle™ is currently made only with U.S. imperial measurements, instructions at the point of making the "bias rectangles" are given only in inches. If you don't have a BiRangle™, there are templates and separate instructions provided.

CUTTING

1 From fabric **A**, cut five 4½ in/11.5 cm strips; subcut to get nine squares 4½ in/11.5 cm wide and 36 rectangles 3½ x 4½ in/9 x 11.5 cm. Trim down the remainder to 2½ in/ 7.5 cm and cut one rectangle 12½ in/31.5 cm long. Cut one 12½ in/31.5 cm strip and subcut into 17 rectangles 12½ x 2½ in/31.5 x 7.5 cm.

2 From fabric **D**, cut two 2½ in/7.5 cm strips and sub-cut into 18 rectangles measuring 2½ x 4½ in/7.5 x 11.5 cm.

3 Using the remainder of fabric **D** and fabrics **B**, **C**, and **F**, cut into 18 in/50 cm pieces. These pieces will be for making the bias rectangle units. The BiRangle™ tool comes with complete instructions which I will not repeat here. You will need to make eight different units as shown below.

54 pieces   **54 pieces**

18 pieces   **18 pieces**   **18 pieces**   **18 pieces**

18 pieces   **18 pieces**

4 Lay fabrics **C** and **D** on top of each other with folds to the left and selvages to the right (shown below).

folds   *selvages*

5 Set up for the BiRangle™ as shown above and use the instructions with the tool to cut both sets of half yards/meters into 3 in strips. Set aside carefully.

6 Use the BiRangle™ similarly for fabrics **D** and **E**. Cut the set into 3 in strips and set aside carefully. Fabrics **B** and **F** will be cut at a later stage.

STITCHING

1 Working with fabrics **C** and **D**, stitch the strips in matching pairs, right sides together, using an exact ¼ in seam. Press carefully. Divide the strips evenly in half.

2 Using the BiRangle™, cut half of the strips, right sides up, into 2½ x 4½ in rectangles. You will need 54 pieces.

3 Use the remaining strips and repeat the process, but with the wrong sides up, to give the slope of the triangle in the opposite direction. Again you will need 54 pieces.

4 Working with the strips from fabrics **D** and **E**, stitch in matching pairs, right sides together, using an exact ¼ in seam. Press carefully. Divide the strips evenly in half.

5 Using the BiRangle™, cut half of the strips, right sides up, into 18 rectangles measuring 2½ x 4½ in. Cut the other half with wrong sides up into 18 more rectangles.

Using templates

1 If you are working in metric or are not using a BiRangle™, use the small pattern (on page 117) for all the above rectangles. Transfer the design onto a piece of cardboard or template plastic. Place the diagonal line of the template on the seam line on the right side for half the set and on the wrong side for the other half.

CUTTING AND STITCHING FABRICS B AND F

1 Set up the two half yards/meters of fabrics **B** and **F** for the BiRangle™ as before. Cut three sets of strips 4 in/10.5 cm wide.

2 Stitch in matching pairs, press carefully and divide into two even groups.

3 Using either the BiRangle™ or the large pattern (on page 117) cut one pieced group, right sides up, into 3½ x 6½ in rectangles. You will need 18 rectangles. Join waste triangles along the bias edge to make up the number. Any waste that is too small can be used later.

4 Using the remaining group, cut rectangles from the stitched strips with the wrong side up. Again you will need 18 large rectangles.

5 Once you have enough large rectangles, cut the remaining fabric at the same angle but 3 in/8 cm wide. Pair and stitch to make small rectangles: 18 with right side facing and 18 with wrong side facing. Waste triangles can be used to complete the number if necessary.

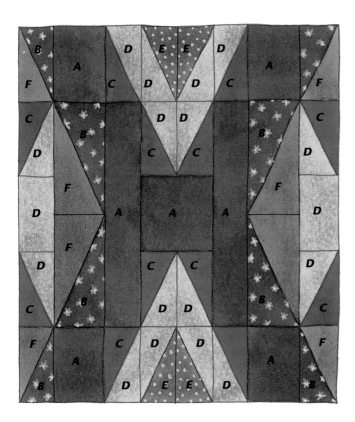

COMPLETING THE BLOCKS

1 Lay out the blocks as shown at left. Stitch the pieces in vertical rows, chain piecing where it will help.

2 Stitch these rows together to form the block. Repeat until you have nine blocks.

FINISHING THE QUILT

1 Lay out the quilt blocks following the quilt plan and stitch together like a large Nine Patch.

2 Layer the backing, batting, and quilt top, pin and baste in a grid from the center out.

3 Quilt in a pattern of your choice. I machine quilted in the ditch, emphasizing the diamonds that are produced when the blocks are joined.

4 When the quilting is completed, join the binding strips as required and use to bind the quilt with double-fold binding.

NIGHT and DAY

Save time in making quilts by not shopping for fabrics; rather dye your own using 100% cotton, several small jars and a packet of cold-water dye. It's a simple process to achieve fabrics that have many color blotches, mottled areas, crinkles, and dye creases. Dyeing becomes more time consuming if an overall even color is required owing to the amount of stirring needed! Stuff the fabric into a bucket or jar for an instant effect! Quilter Vimala McClure calls it "fabric pickling." I've used these color variations to portray different aspects of the countryside, whether it's the approaching night, autumn leaves in dappled midday sunshine, or a lake shimmering in afternoon light.

Three quilts are made using dyed fabric, another is made from acrylic felt, which is hand washable and does not shrink or fray, and the fifth is pieced with both bought and hand-dyed fabrics. All quilts, apart from the crib quilt, have backings that have also been dyed, but a plain or print fabric could be used instead.

You can cut down on the cost of fabric by using worn cotton sheets and dyeing the best pieces. Fabric can be bought that is already prepared for dyeing, but I find that if fabric is first machine washed with soap powder or other detergent, there are no problems. Some shrinkage can occur, and quantities given for each project allow extra for this. Timings given for the quilts do not include the dyeing process.

– CAROL DOWSETT

SQUARE ON SQUARE

This single-bed quilt, based on a 12 in/30 cm block, took approximately fourteen hours to complete. Each block is made from a center square of a star print fabric and four triangles that are cut from two squares. The night sky and its stars are an inspiration in many of my quilts. Some triangles and the backing fabric are dyed as one piece and cut after rinsing, washing, and drying the fabric. If you don't wish to dye your own fabric, there are many predyed fabrics available. The quilt can be made larger or smaller by altering the number of blocks and the placement.

✦

Quilt size: 57½ x 69½ in/145 x 175 cm

MATERIALS

For backing and 40 triangles: prewashed white 100% cotton fabric, 3 yards/2.8 meters, 60 in/150 cm wide
Cold-water dye and fixative: 1 packet dark turquoise; 1 packet fixative
Small bucket
Salt

Dark blue star print fabric: 2 yards/1.9 meters, 45 in/115 cm wide
Cotton print fabric: 5 fat quarters in different reds
Batting: 2 oz, 60 x 72 in/155 x 185 cm
Clear nylon thread for machine quilting
Mercerized cotton for tie quilting

ALTERNATIVE COLOR SCHEMES
By altering the style and coloring of the fabrics, this quilt changes mood and appeal. Clockwise from top left: the jungle print set in plain yellow makes a great design for a child's bed; the two gold star fabrics are more suitable for a teenager; two colors of the same print produce a bright and graphic design for a sunny room; two dark blue prints create a sophisticated look for a modern bedroom.

DYEING USING COLD-WATER DYES

These dyes are safe to use, but, nevertheless, when you are using powdered dye, certain precautions must be taken:

✦ Do not breathe in the dye powder, wear a mask if possible, and have handy a damp cloth to wipe up any spills.

✦ Do not use kitchen utensils you have used for dyeing for any culinary purpose.

✦ Wear rubber gloves and old clothing.

✦ Do not dye fabric near any food or food processing areas.

✦ Cover your work area with plastic sheeting or newspapers.

✦ Dispose of dye liquid in an environmentally safe way.

Basic equipment

✦ jam jars/coffee jars with lids, for small pieces of fabric

✦ kitchen scales

✦ tablespoon

✦ stick for stirring

✦ 2 measuring jugs, for mixing dyes

✦ small bucket, for larger pieces of fabric

For each packet of dye used you will need:

✦ 4 oz/110 g of salt

✦ 1 packet of cold-water-dye fixative

General instructions

Use hot water from the tap and not boiling water. Allow two hours for the dye process to take place.

1 Soak white 100% cotton fabric in cold water, then squeeze out excess. Squash the damp fabric as tightly as possible into a ball and wrap some rubber bands around it or tie up with plastic string.

2 Mix the dye into a measuring jug filled with 20 fl oz/ 500 ml hot water; stir until dissolved. Pour into a small bucket.

3 Mix 4 oz/110 g of salt and the cold-water-dye fixative into a measuring jug filled with 20 fl oz/500 ml hot water; stir until dissolved. Pour into the dye solution in the bucket and stir well.

4 Put the fabric "ball" in the bucket and press down in the dye; stir in just enough cold water added to cover (if needed), and leave for two hours.

5 Empty out the dye and rinse the fabric in warm water until the water runs clear. Wash with non-biological washing powder on a gentle machine cycle, dry and iron.

DYEING

1 Dye the white cotton fabric with the turquoise dye, as described at left.

CUTTING

1 From the dark blue star print fabric, cut twenty 9 in/23 cm squares (shown below).

2 From each fat quarter, cut four 6⅞ in/17.5 cm squares, then cut each square diagonally in half to make a total of eight triangles (shown below). You'll need 40 red triangles.

3 From the hand-dyed turquoise fabric, cut twenty 6⅞ in/ 17.5 cm squares, then cut each square in half to make a total of 40 triangles (shown below).

4 From the remainder of this fabric, cut a rectangle 60 x 72 in/155 x 180 cm for the backing.

backing

5 For the inner border, cut and join together in a random sequence 1½ in/4 cm wide strips of fabric left from the fat quarters.

6 For the outer border, cut and join together 4 in/10 cm wide strips of fabric across the width of the dark blue star print fabric (shown on page 126, top).

7 Cut the remaining dark blue star print into enough 2 in/ 5 cm wide strips to make a double-fold binding to go round the outer edges of the quilt.

STITCHING

1 Using a set of four triangles in the same fabric, stitch a triangle to each side of one 9 in/23 cm star print square using a ¼ in/0.75 cm seam (shown below). Press the seams open.

2 Following the quilt plan, join the blocks together in rows of four blocks each, alternating the dyed fabric blocks with the others. Stitch the rows together.

ADDING THE BORDERS

1 Measure the quilt top across the center from side to side. Cut two strips from the red border fabric to this length. Pin and stitch to the top and bottom of the quilt. Press the seams open.

2 Measure the quilt top across the center from top to bottom. Cut two red border strips to this length, then pin and stitch to the sides of the quilt. Press the seams open.

3 Repeat this process to add the wider dark blue star print strips for the outer border.

FINISHING THE QUILT

1 Lay out the backing, batting, and quilt top and fasten together with safety pins or baste in a grid.

2 Using clear thread on top and regular thread in the bobbin, stitch with a walking foot or even-feed foot in the ditch along all the straight lines.

3 Machine stitch the double binding all round and either machine or hand stitch to the back.

4 Tie the quilt in the center of the squares with a double thread of mercerized cotton.

AUTUMN LEAVES

Dyeing fabric tightly packed into a small space produces wonderful
textures and surprising color variations. Superimposed on this are hand-printed autumn leaf designs
stamped with a simple printing block made from polystyrene or foam, such as the tray that vegetables are sold in from
supermarkets, or use commercial materials that are sold specifically for printing. This combination of hand-dyed fabric
and hand-printed leaves makes a wall hanging or table cover that is evocative of a forest with a floor
of autumnal foliage dappled with sunlight. It took roughly twelve hours.

◆

Quilt size: 48½ x 48½ in/123 x 123 cm

MATERIALS

All fabrics used in the quilt are 60 in/150 cm wide.

Fabric marker
Prewashed white or cream 100% cotton fabric:
2¾ yards/2.5 meters
Backing fabric: 60 x 60 in/150 x 150 cm (use 100%
cotton and dye if desired, or choose a matching brown)
Cold-water dye and fixative: 1 packet brown and 1
packet of fixative for the quilt top, plus same amount for
the backing, if dyeing
Salt and small bucket and stirring stick

Measuring jug and four jam jars with lids
Polystyrene or foam: for making leaf-printing shapes
Knitting needle
Fabric paint: acrylic paint in jars in various colors (I used
burnt umber, metallic copper, pearlescent white, cadmium
yellow)
Paintbrush
Baking parchment paper
Batting: needle-punched, 54 x 54 in/140 x 140 cm
Clear nylon thread for machine quilting
Leaf-shaped sequins or buttons: for tie quilting

CUTTING FOR DYEING

The fabric strips are cut larger than needed to allow for any shrinkage during the dyeing process. Write a number on the jar and a corresponding number in one corner of each strip using the fabric marker.

1 Cut the following across the width of the white or cream cotton fabric:
+ for jar 1, one strip 30 in/80 cm wide
+ for jar 2, one strip 30 in/80 cm wide
+ for jar 3, one strip 22 in/60 cm wide
+ for jar 4, one strip 12 in/30 cm wide
The fabric is subcut once it has been dyed (see below).

DYEING
Quilt backing

1 Follow the instructions given on page 126 to dye the backing fabric with one packet of dye and one packet of fixative, if not using purchased brown fabric.

Quilt top

Check before adding any of the salt, fixative, and dye solution that your jars will be big enough to take the fabric strips plus the total quantity of liquid by testing with the fabric and water, as listed below.

1 Mix 4 oz/110 g salt and one packet of fixative into a measuring jug filled with 20 fl oz/500 ml hot water; stir until dissolved. Divide this equally between the four jars.

2 Mix the contents of one packet of dye in a measuring jug with a small amount of hot water until all dye has dissolved. Add more hot water to make 20 fl oz/500 ml.

3 Divide this between the four jars as follows, stirring the liquid well in each jar:
+ into jar 1 put 4 fl oz/100 ml
+ into jar 2 put 6 fl oz/150 ml
+ into jar 3 put 8 fl oz/200 ml
+ into jar 4 put 2 fl oz/50 ml

4 Add the numbered cut fabric strips to the corresponding jars, pressing them down as tightly as possible with a stick or a spoon. Make sure the fabric in each jar has been covered by the solution – even if only just. Press the fabric down farther rather than add more water. Screw lids on tightly.

5 Leave for two hours, turning each jar three or four times to allow the dye to penetrate different parts of the fabric.

6 Empty the jars and rinse the fabric until the water runs clear. Finish by washing with non-biological washing powder on a cool cycle in the washing machine. Dry and iron.

CUTTING

1 From fabric **1**, cut three **A** squares 8½ in/21.5 cm and two **B** strips 8½ x 24½ in/21.5 x 61.5 cm.

2 From fabric **2**, cut two **C** strips 8½ x 24½ in/21.5 x 61.5 cm and one **D** strip 8½ x 40½ in/21.5 x 101.5 cm.

3 From fabric **3**, cut one **E** strip 8½ x 40½ in/21.5 x 101.5 cm and two **F** strips 4½ x 40½ in/11.5 x 101.5 cm.

4 From fabric **4**, cut two **G** strips 4½ x 48½ in/11.5x 121.5 cm.

5 Cut the pieces of fabric left into strips 2 in/5 cm wide for the binding.

STITCHING

1 Stitch the dyed strips together as shown below. This is a Courthouse Steps variation of Log Cabin patchwork. Use a ¼ in/0.75 cm seam and press all seams open.

PRINTING

1 Trace the leaf shape patterns (at left) and cut out from the polystyrene or foam with scissors. Mark leaf veins with the point of a knitting needle.

2 Attach a rolled piece of masking tape to the back of each leaf block to make a handle.

3 Put the paint directly onto the print block using a paintbrush. Combine two colors and try printing on scrap dyed fabric first. When you have perfected your technique, print the leaves in groups, across any seam lines, making each a slightly different color. Allow the paint to dry, then iron on a hot setting using baking parchment paper to protect the fabric.

FINISHING THE QUILT

1 Lay out the backing, batting, and quilt top and fasten together with safety pins or baste in a grid system.

2 Using clear thread on top and regular thread in the bobbin, stitch in the ditch along all the straight lines. Trim the excess batting and backing level with the quilt top.

3 Stitch the binding strips together to make the length required and use to bind the quilt with a double-fold binding.

4 Tie-quilt with leaf-shaped sequins or buttons placed at random all over the quilt.

AUTUMN LEAVES PATTERNS

SHIMMERING WATER

*Using a combination of dyeing and fabric painting, this wall hanging shows a scene
of thick bulrushes beside a sunlit lake. It took about ten hours. To give more of a shimmer to the golden water,
strips of fraying metallic fabrics are stitched with utility quilting stitches. The bulrushes are printed on and
fraying fabrics are stitched down in between to add a feeling of depth to the picture.*

◆

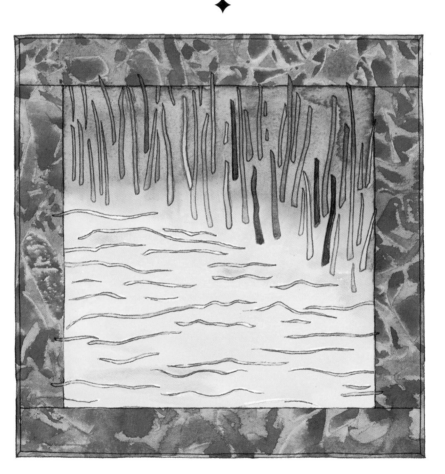

Quilt size: 36 x 36 in/90 x 90 cm

MATERIALS

Prewashed white 100% cotton fabric: 2.5 yards/
2.3 meters, 60 in/150 cm wide for both quilt top and
backing
Cold-water dye and fixative: 1 packet each yellow and
bronze-rose; 2 packets fixative
Salt
2 measuring jugs and stirring stick
Plastic sheeting
1½ in/4 cm household paintbrush

Small bucket
Small strips of polystyrene or foam: for printing
Fabric paint: acrylic in jars in various colors
(I used burnt umber, pearlescent white, and metallic copper.)
Baking parchment paper
Batting: needle-punched, 40 x 40 in/100 x 100 cm
Small pieces of sheer, metallic, and glitzy fabrics
Embroidery thread: fine cotton to match the color range
used in the hanging

CUTTING

1 Cut a 32 in/80 cm square from one corner of the white cotton fabric for the quilt top (shown below, right) and leave the cutting of the rest until after it has been dyed.

PAINTING AND DYEING
Painting the water scene

1 Dissolve the yellow dye into 5 fl oz/150 ml of hot water.

2 Mix 4 oz/110 g salt and one packet of fixative into 10 fl oz/300 ml hot water, then combine in a jug with the dye mixture.

3 Mix the bronze-rose dye separately, using the same recipe, and put into a separate jug – do not combine the two colors.

4 Dampen the 32 in/80 cm square of fabric, then place on the plastic sheeting and smooth out.

5 Dip the paintbrush into the yellow dye and paint the bottom half of the water scene as shown on the quilt plan. Paint more dye onto some areas to alter the depth of color.

6 With the bronze-rose dye and a clean brush, paint the top half of the fabric, letting the two colors run into each other and again going over some areas so that they will be a stronger shade. Work as quickly as possible – it doesn't matter how wet the fabric becomes!

7 Place a piece of plastic on top (to aid "curing") and leave at least two hours – preferably overnight, then rinse, wash in non-biological washing powder, dry, and iron.

Dyeing the borders and backing

1 As soon as you have finished dye painting, dampen the remaining fabric and squash it into a small bucket.

2 Pour the remaining bronze-rose dye mixture slowly and directly onto the fabric, moving the fabric around with a stick or a gloved hand to make sure the dye gets to most areas. Push tightly into a ball.

3 Pour on the remaining yellow dye mixture slowly as before. Scrunch the ball tightly down to soak up all the dye. If you feel that there is not enough liquid, add a little cold water. Leave for two hours, then rinse, wash in non-biological washing powder, dry, and iron.

CUTTING

1 Trim the water scene to a square 28½ in/71.5 cm.

2 From the dyed fabric, cut two 4¼ x 28½ in/ 10.75 x 71.5 cm strips for the sides; two 4¼ x 36 in/ 10.75 x 90 cm strips for the top and bottom (shown below).

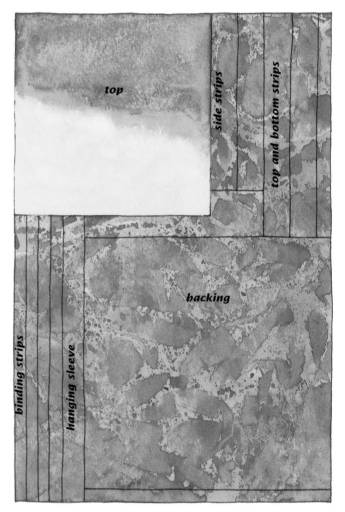

3 For the backing, cut a 40 in/100 cm square (shown above).

4 For the double-fold binding, cut strips 2 in/5 cm wide and long enough when joined to go all around the hanging (shown above).

5 For the hanging sleeve, cut a strip 7½ x 36 in/19 x 90 cm.

STITCHING AND PRINTING

1 Stitch on the side strips first, matching centers, and press the seams toward the outer edges.

2 Stitch on the top and bottom strips and press the seams as before.

3 Trace the bulrush printing shape patterns (at right) and cut these out from the polystyrene or foam. Attach a rolled piece of masking tape to the back of each block to make a handle.

4 Put fabric paint onto the shapes and print over the top half of the water scene – try this out first on scrap dyed fabric to test the colors and the technique (see page 131). Combine paint colors. Use the edges and flat surface of the print blocks to vary the shapes, and lean some at different angles into the side borders (see quilt plan). Use the white pearlescent paint on a brush to make areas of shimmer on the water. Let the paint dry, then iron, using baking parchment paper to protect the fabric surface.

FINISHING THE QUILT

1 Layer the backing, batting, and quilt top and fasten together with safety pins or baste into a grid system.

2 Cut narrow strips of sheer, metallic, and glitzy fabrics on the bias (this slows down the fraying); place either on top or to one side of the printed shapes and stitch with utility quilting stitches (see page 62) through the center of each. Quilt some lines without fabric strips. Use these techniques for the shimmering water also.

3 Stitch on the 2 in/5 cm double-fold binding and attach a hanging sleeve.

SHIMMERING WATER
BULRUSH PATTERNS

DAWN

To perfect a fabric that has glimpses of different blues, from palest to darkest, that evoke the lightening of the night sky is surprisingly simple to achieve using cold-water dyes. This technique uses tightly scrunched-up fabric, tied into a ball, then immersed in just enough dye solution to cover it. The very center of this ball will absorb only a little dye liquid and other areas more. The fabric is dyed before it is cut for the quilt. This quilt is based on a 12 in/30 cm block and is designed as a single-bed quilt. By altering the number of blocks and keeping the same width border strips, any size quilt can be made. This quilt took about twenty hours.

◆

Quilt size: 60 x 84 in/150 x 210 cm

MATERIALS

Prewashed white 100% cotton fabric: 4 yards/ 3.6 meters, 60 in/150 cm wide
Rubber bands or plastic string
Cold-water dye and fixative: 1 packet each of dark blue and yellow-orange; 2 packets fixative
2 measuring jugs and stirring stick
2 small buckets
Salt
Backing: 100% cotton, 2½ yards/2.3 meters, 90 in/

230 cm wide. (If you wish to dye this fabric, use 1 packet of dark blue and 1 packet of fixative; use the general dyeing instructions given on page 126.)
Batting: cotton, 64 x 88 in/160 x 220 cm
Machine-quilting thread in blue and orange
Thin cardboard to make star template
Acrylic felt: dark blue, 18 in/50 cm, 36 in/90 cm wide
Freezer paper for appliqué stars
Baking parchment paper

DYEING

Cut the white cotton fabric in half crosswise to make two pieces 2 yards/1.8 meters long. Dye one blue and the other yellow-orange, as described below.

1 Dampen the pieces of fabric, then squash each into a tight ball. Tie around with rubber bands or plastic string.

2 Mix the contents of each packet of dye into 20 fl oz/500 ml of hot water in a measuring jug, and pour each into a small bucket. Mix 4 oz/110 g salt and one packet of fixative into 20 fl oz/500 ml of hot water in a measuing jug. Add to one of the buckets and stir well. Repeat for the second bucket.

3 Add one ball of fabric to each bucket and push it around and under the dye with a stick to get it saturated with the solution. Add a little more cold water if necessary. Leave for two hours, then rinse, wash in non-biological washing powder, dry, and iron.

CUTTING

1 Following the cutting plan below, left, from the blue fabric, cut eight 12½ in/31.5 cm squares, eight 6½ in/16.5 cm squares, two 6½ x 36½ in/16.5 x 91.5 cm rectangles, and four 6½ x 30½ in/16.5 x 76.5 cm strips. Join these last four strips into pairs with a ¼ in/0.75 cm seam to make two strips 6½ x 60½ in/16.5 x 151.5 cm.

2 Cut the same from the orange fabric, except you need only seven 12½ in/31.5 cm squares. Join the strips as before.

STITCHING

1 Referring to the quilt plan, stitch the large squares into rows, then stitch the rows together. Press the seams open.

2 Stitch pairs of rectangles together, one orange to one blue, following the quilt plan.

3 Stitch the longer rectangles to the quilt top sides, matching centers.

4 Stitch together the smaller squares into sets of four and stitch these to each end of the shorter rectangles. Attach these to both ends of the quilt. Press all the seams open.

FINISHING THE QUILT

1 Layer the backing, batting, and quilt top and fasten together with safety pins or baste into a grid system.

2 Machine quilt with blue thread in straight lines 1 in/2.5 cm on either side of each seam line.

3 Trace the larger star pattern **D** on page 139 and glue it to the cardboard. Mark around it randomly onto the quilt top 10 to 21 times (depending on time available) and stitch on the marked lines with orange thread.

4 Trace the smaller star pattern **C** on page 139 and cut out 10 to 21 stars from freezer paper. Iron these onto the felt, using baking parchment paper to protect the fabric. Cut out the felt stars, then remove the freezer paper. Pin these felt stars inside the quilted star motifs and stitch down with blue thread using a straight stitch.

5 Trim the batting to the same size as the quilt top and trim the backing 1 in/2.5 cm bigger all round. Turn in ½ in/1 cm and fold over onto the quilt top. Machine stitch in place.

DAWN AND CATCH A FALLING STAR PATTERNS

*Instructions for using the "Dawn" patterns
below appear on page 138.
Instructions for using the "Catch a Falling Star"
patterns below appear on page 142.*

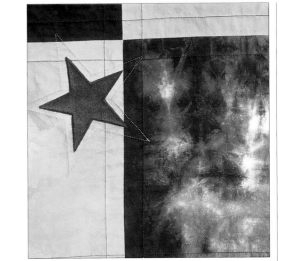

A = small star (Catch a Falling Star)
B = medium star (Catch a Falling Star)
C = small star (Dawn)
D = large star (Catch a Falling Star and Dawn)

A
B
C
D

CATCH A FALLING STAR

This small quilt is made using two layers of washable acrylic felt, without batting. Patterns cut from felt do not fray and can be stitched in place without a turning. I machine stitched throughout and the quilt took roughly eight hours to make. This felt is not suitable for constant washing, but the quilt could be used more as a decorative top for a baby carriage or crib. By adding a hanging sleeve, it could be used as a nursery wall hanging.

◆

Quilt size: 24 x 34 in/60 x 90 cm

MATERIALS

Acrylic felt (for the top, backing, and some stars):
pale yellow, 1¼ yards/115 cm; bright yellow,
1 yard/90 cm; blue, 12 in/30 cm, all 36 in/90 cm wide
Thin cardboard for star templates
Two cotton printed star fabrics for the large stars:
one 8 in/20 cm square from each fabric
Fusible webbing: 8 x 16 in/20 x 40 cm

Thick topstitching thread: pale yellow, bright yellow,
and blue to match the colors of the felt
Freezer paper for appliqué stars
Baking parchment paper
Rayon machine thread: in colors to match the printed
star fabrics
Regular sewing thread: in colors to match the
topstitching thread and the rayon machine thread

CUTTING

1 From the pale yellow felt, cut a 34 x 24 in/90 x 60 cm rectangle for the backing.

2 Cut a rectangle the same size from the bright yellow felt for the top layer.

3 Trace the three star patterns (**A**, **B**, and **D)** on page 139 and glue them onto cardboard to use as templates.

4 From the blue felt, cut eight small stars (**A**) and six medium stars (**B**).

5 From bright yellow felt, cut four small stars and four medium stars.

6 From the pale yellow felt, cut eight small stars and eight medium stars.

7 From each of the star fabrics, cut one large star (**D**), then iron fusible webbing onto both stars.

STITCHING

1 Baste the two rectangles of felt together and, using matching topstitching thread, stitch two rows around the edges, the first row $^1/_8$ in/4 mm from the edge and the second $^3/_8$ in/1 cm from the edge as shown on the quilt plan.

2 Draw round the large star template onto freezer paper and cut out five stars. Following the quilt plan or in your own arrangement, iron them onto the quilt top, using baking parchment paper to protect the felt. Stitch around the papers using the thicker thread to match the bright yellow felt, then remove the paper.

3 Place the two large fabric stars, just slightly offset from the stitching, as shown on the quilt plan. Iron in place, protecting the surface with baking parchment paper.

4 Satin stitch by machine around the two stars using a rayon thread, or attach by hand with buttonhole stitch.

5 Place the small and medium felt stars at random over the top, trying not to overlap, securing each with a pin.

6 With a darning foot and feed dog down, on each of the stars stitch a spiral from the center outward using a contrasting topstitching thread (shown above, right).

7 Using regular matching colored sewing thread, stitch down each star with a straight machine stitch around the edges.

FINISHING THE QUILT

1 Using baking parchment paper to protect the surface, press with a cool iron.

2 Whenever necessary, wash the quilt gently in warm water and dry flat.

USEFUL ADDRESSES

SPECIALTY SUPPLIERS

Dylon International
Prym-Dritz Corporation
P O Box 5028
Spartanburg, SC 29304
(For dyes and fixative)

Liquitex
Binney and Smith Inc.
1100 Church Lane
P O Box 431
Easton, PA 18044-0431
(For acrylic fabric paints)

Sanford Berol
Pencil Street
Shelbyville, TN 37160
(For Pressprint & Easiprint: fabric
printing blocks)

That Patchwork Place, Inc
P O Box 118
Bothell, WA 98041 - 0118
(For the BiRangle™)

MAIL ORDER QUILTING SOURCES

The following mail-order sources carry a
broad range of sewing and quilting
supplies, notions, tools, and equipment.
Call or write for catalogs – most are free.

U.S.A.

Atlanta Thread & Supply Company
695 Red Oak Road
Stockbridge, GA 30281
800-847-1001

Calico Corners
203 Gale Lane
Kennett Square, PA 19348
800-777-9933

Clothilde Inc.
2 Sew Smart Way B8032
Stevens Point, WI 54481
800-772-2891

Keepsake Quilting
Route 25B
P.O. Box 1618
Centre Harbor, NH 03226
800-865-9458

Newark Dressmaker Supply
6473 Ruch Road
P.O. Box 20730
Lehigh Valley, PA 18002
800-736-6783

Oppenheim's
P.O. Box 29
120 East Main Street
North Manchester, IN 46962
800-461-6728

Quilts and Other Comforts
6700 W. 44th Avenue
P.O. Box 394
Wheat Ridge, CO 80034
303-420-4270

Sew/Fit Company
P.O. Box 397
Bedford Park, IL 60499
800-547-4739

The Stearns Technical Textile Co.
100 Williams Street
Cincinnati, OH 45215
800-354-7150
(For batting)

Canada

Calico Cupboard
5325 Cordova Bay Rd
Victoria, BC V8Y 2L3
604-658-2722

Homespun Craft Emporium
250A 2nd Avenue S
Saskatoon, SK S7K 1K9
306-652-3585

La Maison de Calico
324 Lakeshore Blvd
Pointe Claire, QC H9S 4L7
514-695-0728

Quilters' Fancy Ltd.
2877 Bloor Street W
Toronto, ON M8X 1B3
416-232-1199

Quilters' Quarters
595 Mt. Pleasant
Toronto, ON M4S 2M5
416-487-1047

The Cloth Shop
4415 West 10th Avenue
Vancouver, BC V6R 2HB
604-224-132

The Cotton Patch
1717 Bedford Hwy
Bedford, NS B4W 1X3
902-861-2782

The Fabric Cottage
16 Crowfood Terrace NW
Calgary, AB T3G 4J8
403-241-3070

The Quilter's Cabin
118-10816 MacLeod Trail S
Calgary, AB T2J 5N8
403-278-4433

The Quilter's Hope Chest
2483 Agricola
Halifax, NS B3K 4C3
902-425-5002

The Quilting Bee
1026 St. Mary's Rd
Winnipeg, MB R2M 3S6
204-254-7870

ACKNOWLEDGMENTS

Quilters often rely on the pioneering
work of others in developing new ideas.
We would like to thank those who have
kindly given us permission to reproduce
their designs:

Patchwork Quilt Tsushin for
permission to use Sawako Tsurugiji's
kimono block design in Jenni Dobson's
"Pacific Kimono."

That Patchwork Place for allowing us
to use the quilting stitches in Gill
Turley's Decorative Stitches Sampler. The
quilting stitch patterns are copyrighted
designs by Judy D. Hopkins and appear
in *Rotary Riot* by Judy Hopkins and
Nancy J. Martin, published by That
Patchwork Place, 1991. They also
produce the BiRangle™.

INDEX